Published by Aperitifs Publishing Company
Santa Rosa, California

Copyright: March 2022

Written by:
John C. Burton
johncburton@msn.com
707-523-1611

Bob Welch
Santacruzbrews@yahoo.com

Library of Congress Number: 2022902448
ISBN: 978-1-7324530-4-3
Printed in the United States of America

All rights reserved. No part of this book may be reproduced or transformed in any form or by any means, electronic or mechanical, including photocopying, recording or by any information storage and/or retrieval system without permission in writing from the author or publisher. Every attempt has been made to provide accurate information on the following subjects.

ACKNOWLEDGEMENTS

John Burton for assisting me in putting together this book that I have dreamed about for quite some time. With our numerous emails, phone calls and text messages through the months since October 2021 we have put together a book that we feel is desirable to collectors of California paper labels and paper label bottles. He has my gratitude and we both look forward to following up with volume two in the future.

Thomas Jacobs for his addition to this endeavor with his knowledge and history of how these labels were applied to bottles prior to Prohibition. It's fascinating to understand the development of labeling of bottles; something we take for granted as we pass thru the aisles of stores today.

Bob Kay and his son Forrest Kay for helping me fill in the remainder of my California label collection and being a major influence in my label collecting though the years. The Kay's were always courteous when assisting me in selection of filling in the gaps of my collection. To them, a special Thank You.

Sarah Trejo for assisting us with assembling the material and putting it in an orderly manner. Sarah has been instrumental in putting together each of my books (John Burton) and sending them to my publisher. Always comfortable when working with a professional.

BOB WELCH COLLECTION OF CALIFORNIA
PRE-PROHIBITION, PROHIBITION AND CALIFORNIA PERMIT & IRTP PAPER BEER BOTTLES AND LABELS

I've been collecting most of my life, as like many my age, starting with stamps, and then selling my collection when I was 18 years old to purchase my first car, a 1974 Monte Carlo, Gold color with off white vinal top.

In the late 1980's having a passion for beer and brewing I began to focus on collecting California Brewery related items. I made a point of collecting anything California, pre-Prohibition to 1950.

This book shows many of the beer bottles and labels I have acquired thru the years. I made a point of collecting any label or labeled bottle that I did not have in my collection. At the time I collected items in any condition upgrading thru the years.

Most bottles and labels were acquired at flea markets, antique bottle shows, beer can shows and purchasing from fellow collectors including many key labels from Bob Kay's collection. And yes, the internet has come into play.

The main focus of this book is to share and show examples of the majority of California paper beer labels and bottles in my collection. Thank You;

                                                        Bob Welch

Forward

I was excited when John Burton told me he was writing a book on beer labels with Bob Welch. As a long time collector of "beers" I am entering my 55th year of collecting and have seen collectors come and go and the category of breweriana change dramatically. I remember when Bob was a "rookie", just starting out. When I became aware of this groundbreaking work I asked John, like Bob, a longtime friend, if I could write a forward.

Most of us started as just bottle collectors, searching for bottles with embossing to line up on a shelf, looking for the next example that we didn't have. Non-bottle items would show up at shows and were not paid much attention to. Collectors called these things "go-withs". Though inexpensive I passed up the "go-withs" saving my limited capital for the glass. I felt etched glasses were not worth more than $5 but did buy my first National AD. Lang glass for $8, feeling that I paid too much.

First show I attended in San Mateo in 1967, I passed on a labeled Fredericksburg miniature for $25, (too much!) but did buy a green whittled Lutge quart for $8. Beers where cheap, splits $3, pints $5, and quarts $5. The Lutge being colored was worth an extra $3. At that show I remember a "Tony Phillips" for $13 (outrageous I thought, looks too much like a John Rapp) I never thought much of the Lutge I did buy because it was so cheap and easy and no one else scooped it up.

Everyone in those days had a "specialty" in bottles. My friend Earl specialized in beers and had a dozen lined up on his shelf. They looked good. I decided on beers myself because, unlike whiskeys or bitters, they were affordable for a teenager and were bottles we would "dig" in Marin County, a 19th and early 20th century picnic area where beer bottles, which had a deposit, were thrown away rather than carried back.

I met Bill and Audrey Willis who were selling bottles at the Cow Palace Flea Market, later visiting their home in Belmont and buying enough beers to streak past Earl's smaller grouping. I haven't looked back, at one time narrowing down to just San Francisco but expanding back to California when given the chance to buy the best all California collection. I now have over 900 bottles, two-thirds being San Francisco.

So, what do you do when you are not getting many new bottles? Suddenly the go-withs and researching history becomes a pursuit that adds interest to a collection. Labels are history and with Bob's focus a category.

What I have seen in my years of collecting is collectors concentrating on specific segments of breweriana as prices of more desirable and unattainable items escalate. Prices of these lesser items start to escalate themselves as collectors compete for them. Suddenly foam scrapers, classically priced at $5 or less, escalate to over $100 or more, becoming less available. Even marked patented stoppers have made a run out of the 25-cent box. Bob Welch has become the "label guy" and since that dedication I can't recall adding a good label to my collection. Bob has laser focus and moves quickly at the shows I am immediately cornered, as a known experienced collector, by those wanting their items evaluated for value and rarity. I am also looking at everything on tables instead of having a single item I am looking for like Bob.

Labels on high value bottles in the early days could be endangered, especially if the glass was beautiful when illuminated from behind. To some, labels just got in the way of enjoying the glass, which was the important thing, and were washed off. Years ago, I bought Dave Streit's better bottles. One was a stunning honey amber Roeschman (embossed bear) quart. After the sale Dave gave me the label he soaked off that bottle. Didn't come off perfectly but at least it was preserved. This is how labels were treated.

Occasionally a labeled example would come along. I had a rule that I would pay a maximum $5 more that the value of the embossed bottle to get one with a label. With that rule I missed some great labels. I did get a nice Gambrinus Bottling Co. in the late '60's. It was a worthless "no name" turn mold. Fit my rule, paid $5. Great graphic label with a German bar maid, glass mugs and bottle in hands, rolling on a beer barrel in water as a lumberjack would roll on a log.

This label, dating from the early '90's may be the only physical remnant of this bottling works which was not connected with the later Gambrinus Bottling Co. Also, unlike Gambrinus Bottling Co., that bottled beer from the brewery of the same name in Portland, Oregon. This bottler bottled, as stated on the label, Fredericksburg Lager Beer. And this points to the value of labels over embossed bottles.

Years ago, I got a grouping of labeled San Francisco quarts. They were found wrapped in rags in a box under a house with a note stating they were consumed by a young man on his 21st birthday. In the group were two "3B Beer" labels, on one a D. Meinke bottle and the other a rare embossed 3B San Francisco bottle. This associated both of these bottles, the 3B with Meinke, and the Meinke with the Bellingham Bay Brewery beer. Also in the group were two embossed North Star Bottling Works bottles both with different labels. The works was on 26th Street right behind the North Star Brewery on Army Street. Both labels indicate they were bottling beer from the Chicago Brewery across town on Pine Street. Who knew or would suspect going by the embossing? A label tells a true story. These later labels also have telephone numbers which changed so frequently they can be used with old telephone directories to date the label and bottle.

I have had a chance to research trademark court cases where one brewer sues another or a bottler for imitating their label. Fred Kostering (Los Angeles Bottling Co. SF) was sued for imitating the Rainier beer label. Kostering's label at a distance looked exactly like the Rainier label with some colors and general graphic design.

Arthur Guinness and Sons sued a number of San Francisco Brewers and beer bottlers, Enterprise Brewing Co. and Daniel Tweedie among them, for imitating their trademarked label with a serial number. American Brewing Co. of Berkeley was sued by American Brewing Company of St. Louis for using the term "ABC Beer". The Berkeley Brewery owned by Joseph Raspiller, then changed its name to "Raspiller Brewing Co."

When you own a lot of "stuff" you own pieces of an industry and interest naturally gravitates to how business was conducted. Most of the paper advertising, signs, calendars, and labels were created by a" stone lithographic" process where a multi-colored image is created by multiple pressings under inked lithographic stones. The quality and depth of an image has no modern process that can compare, making early lithography a thing of beauty.

Even how labels were applied to the bottles is of interest. I had a chance in the late 1970's to interview, and tape record, Charlie Dechent, whose father, Charles Dechent, Sr. ran the City Bottling Co. on Pt. Lobos Avenue in San Francisco. Charlie worked with his father in the basement bottling works and knew, as a participant, every part of the small operation. I asked Charlie how the labels were put on the bottles. He told me they painted a board with tragacanth paste then laid the labels in the paste, peeling them up and applying them to the bottles.

This method is detailed in "The Beer Bottler's Handy Book" by Phillip Dreesbach circa 1906. The method is discouraged because the neatness of the bottle of beer was the ultimate goal. Hand application was also discouraged because the label may be crooked or rumpled and smeared with paste. Dreesbach talks about labeling machines used by larger bottling works.

To quote, "The general advantages to be derived from the use of automatic labeling machines are speed of operation, little experience of the operator being necessary to properly run the machine, cleanliness of the finished bottle since no paste can get upon the label or hands of the operator, labels are all fixed uniformly; that is at equal height from and to the lower edge parallel to the bottom of the bottle, or if slanting labels are used, the slant of all labels is of the same angle."

Advertisements for these machines appear in brewing and bottling trade journals. They appear to be motor driven and once a bottle is inserted actuated by depressing a foot pedal.

I write this in advance of seeing the final product (book) but having seen and purchased some of Bob Welch's high-quality label blow-up reproductions; I look forward to a groundbreaking work with page after page of discoveries and information new to me. John Burton will be able to add to his prodigious legacy of putting together books that catalogue bottles and collectibles, presenting them to collectors and the general public, that would otherwise not know what exists.

Thomas Jacobs

San Rafael, California

LABEL IDENTIFICATION

Collecting paper labels is like walking through history; the labels tell you a story, more so than embossed bottles that have limited information. Paper labels can provide brewery information regarding alcohol content, brewery permit number, Internal Revenue Tax Paid, net contents, maybe the union bug, and of course the brand, the brewery and/or bottler and possibly street address. And of course, great graphic art which is never found on embossed bottle.

FEDERAL PERMITS

Brewery permits were required on labels from 1926 to 1936. Most likely the permits were to control taxes on the beer.

CEREAL BEVERAGE

Cereal Beverage labels were required in 1916 to state ½% alcohol-by-volume, name of the bottler and/or distributor and type of cereal product.

A-PERMITS

A Permits were for Medicinal Beer from 1920-1921 that could be purchased by prescription from your doctor or dentist. Normal prescription fee was two dollars. Wording on the label had to read *"For Medicinal Purposes Only. Sale or use for any other purpose will cause will heavy penalties to be inflicted."*

H PERMITS

H Permits were for Malt Extract and Tonic Elixir products sold in drug stores for medicinal puurposes from 1920 -1933 during Prohibition. The labels on H-Permit bottles claimed strengthening the nervous system, good indigestion, and encourageing the appetite. Most neglected to mention that when adding alcohol it was a form of beer.

L-PERMITS

L-Permits were required from 1926-1933 on labels of surplus grain alcohol that could be spiked. The product started out as beer, then the alcohol was removed and the consumer could add their own alcohol to the grain.

U-PERMITS

U-Permits were required from 1933-1936 by the Department of Treasury, Bureau of Alcohol, Tobacco & Firearms after Prohibition was repealed. Originally for tax control of 3.2% beer and new start-up brewers.

INTERNAL REVENUE TAX PAID

Mention of IRTP on labels was required with the ending of U-Permits in June 1935 until March 1950. The IRTP stamped on the label showed that the Federal Tax had been paid prior to being released to a distributor.

ABBREVIATIONS

PP - Pre-Prohibition   P – Prohibition   IRTP – Internal Revenue Tax Paid

LET THE LABEL SPEAK TO YOU

Labels: TEMPORARY LABEL, Brand Name, PERCENTAGE OF ALCOHOL, CA. PERMIT, CONTENTS, BOTTLING CO., ADDRESS & CITY, IRTP, UNION BUG

Controlled By Department of the Treasury, Bureau of Alcohol and Firearms
Statement on Mission Malt Tonic reason 1906 Pure Food & Advertising Law came into effect

GUARANTEED UNDER PURE FOOD AND DRUGS ACT JUNE 30, 1906

TEMPERANCE
BEER WAS AVAILABLE BY PRESCRIPTION ONLY
Required an A Permit
Circa 1920 – 1921

EXTRACTS & TONICS
H Permit
Not Over 2% alcohol by volume
1920's – 1933

NEAR-BEER & CEREAL BEVERAGES
L-1 Permit
1926 – 1933
½% by volume

3.2% BEER
1933 – September 1935
CA. Permit U-1112
IRTP

IRTP
Internal Revenue Tax Paid
1933 – March 1950
Federal tax being paid prior to beer removed from brewery

Printers Proof Label
Notice alignment (+) on center of top, bottom and both sides
Label would be reversed when printing

Label with Perforations
Holes punched into label to reveal date brewed
Amberlite Temperance Beer 12.26.15

ANAHEIM – UNION BREWING CO.
1904 – 1920
Top Image Postcard
Labels Pre-Prohibition

BAKERSFIELD – BAKERSFIELD BREWING CO.
1911 - 1920
Top Label Pre-Prohibition
Bottom Label Prohibition

IRTP

Pre-Prohibition

BAKERSFIELD – KERN BREWING CO.
1938 - 1939
Labels IRTP

BERKELEY – (West Berkeley) RASPILLAR BREWING CO.
1902 - 1910
Labels Pre-Prohibition

RASPILLER BREWING CO. WEST BERKELEY, CAL.

ETNA MILLS – ETNA BREWERY
1867 - 1920
Label Pre-Prohibition
Bottom Image Postcard

Picking hops in California

EUREKA – HUMBOLDT BREWING CO.
1903 – 1920
Label Pre-Prohibition

Pre-Prohibition

Pre-Prohibition

Pre-Prohibition

Pre-Prohibition

EUREKA – HUMBOLDT BREWING CO
1903 - 1920
Label Pre-Prohibition

EUREKA – HUMBOLDT MALT & BREWING CO.
1933 - 1940
Label CA. L-Permit and CA.U-Permit

CA. U-Permit

CA. U-Permit

CA. U-Permit

CA. U-Permit

EUREKA – HUMBOLDT MALT & BREWING CO.
1933 - 1940
CA Permit U-1121

CA. U-Permit

CA. U-Permit

CA. U-Permit CA. U-Permit

CA. U-Permit

EUREKA – HUMBOLDT MALT & BREWING CO.
1933 - 1940

CA. U-Permit

CA. U-Permit

CA. U-Permit

CA. U-Permit

CA. U-Permit

FRESNO – FRESNO BREWING CO.
1900 – 1920
Labels Pre-Prohibition

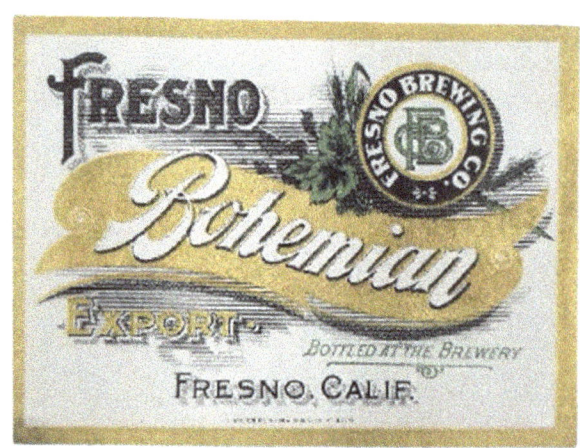

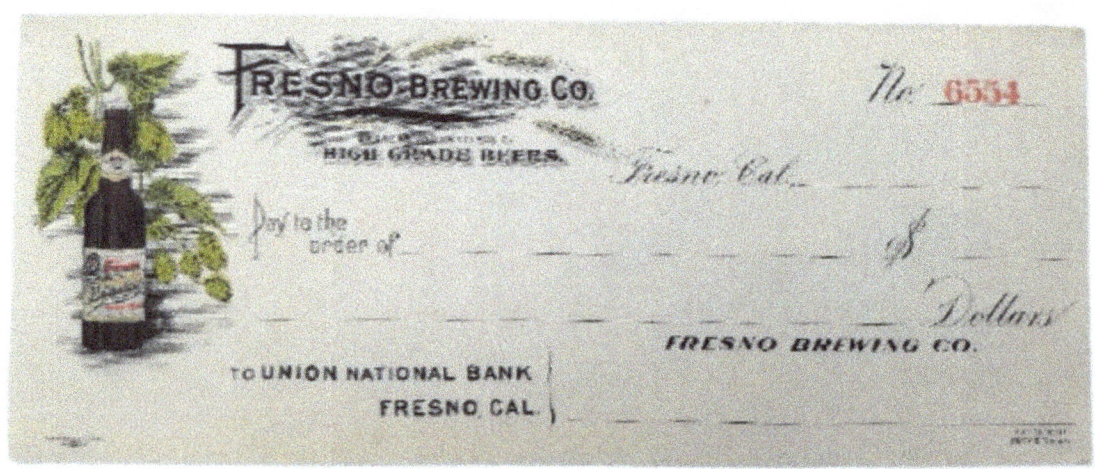

FRESNO – FRESNO BREWING CO.
1900 – 1920
1920 – 1933 (Prohibition)
1933 - 1942
Label CA. U-Permit

Pre-Prohibition

CA. U-Permit

CA. U-Permit

Prohibition

FRESNO – FRESNO BREWING CO.
1900 – 1920
1920 – 1933 (Prohibition)
1933 - 1942

CA. U-Permit

CA. U-Permit

CA. U-Permit

IRTP

CA. U-Permit

CA. U-Permit

FRESNO – GRACE BROS. LTD.
1942 - 1949
Label IRTP

IRTP

IRTP

IRTP

FRESNO – YOSEMITE BREWING CO.
1934 - 1939
Top Label CA. U-Permit
Bottom Label IRTP

HOLLYWOOD – KOCH BREWING CO. INC.
1934 – 1934
Top Label CA. U-Permit
LOS ANGELES – COMET DISTRIBUTING CO.
1934 - 1935
Bottom Label CA. U-Permit

LOS ANGELES – HOLLYWOOD BREWING CO.
1934 – 1935
Top Label CA. U-Permit
Formerly Koch Brewing Co. Inc.
1934 – 1934
Bottom Label CA. U-Permit

IRTP

IRTP

JACKSON – JOHN STROHM BREWERY
1884 - 1920
Label Pre-Prohibition

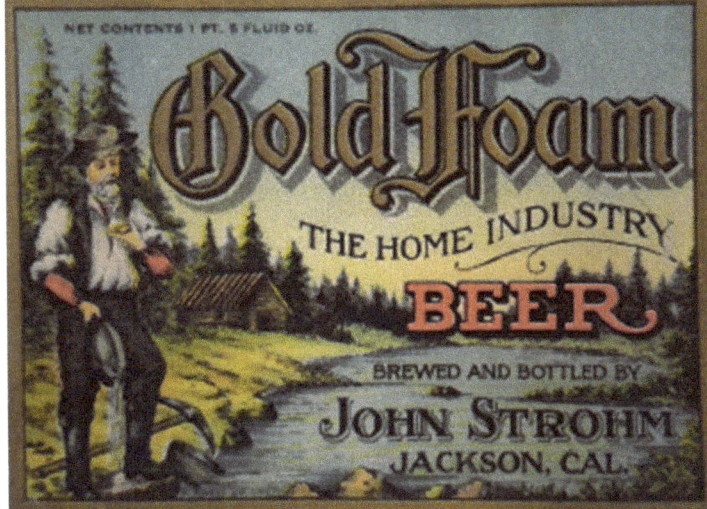

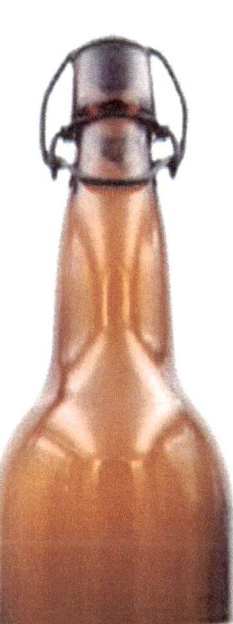

Pre-Prohibition

Pre-Prohibition

Pre-Prohibition

LOS ANGELES – ACME BREWING CO.
Branch of San Francisco
1935 - 1954
Labels IRTP

LOS ANGELES – ACME BREWING CO.
Branch of San Francisco
1935 - 1954
Top Label IRTP
Bottom Label CA. U-Permit

LOS ANGELES – AMBASSADOR BREWING CO.
1933 - 1940
Label IRTP

CA. U-Permit

IRTP

IRTP

CA. U-Permit

LOS ANGELES – AMBASSADOR BRWING CO.
1933 - 1940
Label CA. U-Permit

CA. U-Permit

CA. U-Permit

CA. U-Permit

Center Bottle Half Gallon Picnic
CA. U-Permit

CA. U-Permit

LOS ANGELES – AMBASSADOR BREWING CO.
1933 - 1940
Top Labels IRTP
Bottom Label CA. U-Permit

LOS ANGELES – BALBOA BREWING CO.
Formerly Mathie Brewing Co.
1933 - 1937
Label CA. U-Permit

CA. U-Permit

CA. U-Permit

CA. U-Permit

LOS ANGELES - ECKERTS BREWING CO.
1934 - 1943
Both Labels CA. U-Permit

CA. U-Permit

CA. U-Permit
Painted Label

CA. U-Permit
Painted Label

LOS ANGELES – STEWART McKEE & CO.
Formerly Eckerts Brewing Co
1943 - 1948
Label IRTP

IRTP

IRTP

IRTP

LOS ANGELES – GRACE BROS. LTD.
1937 - 1951
AKA Southern Brewery
1940's - 1951

IRTP

IRTP

IRTP

IRTP

IRTP

IRTP

LOS ANGELES – GRACE BROS. LTD.
1937 - 1951
AKA Southern Brewery
1940's - 1951
Label IRTP

IRTP

IRTP

IRTP

IRTP

IRTP

LOS ANGELES – GRACE BROS. LTD.
1937 – 1951
AKA Southern Brewery
1940's - 1951
Labels IRTP

LOS ANGELES – GRACE BROS. LTD.
1937 - 1951
AKA Southern Brewery
1940's - 1951

IRTP

IRTP

IRTP

LOS ANGELES – MT. BALDY BREWING CO.
Bottled by Gutsch Brewing Co. Inc.
Top Label CA. U-Permit

LOS ANGELES – MT. WILSON BREWING CO.
Bottled by Gutsch Brewing Co. Inc.
Label CA. U-Permit

SANTA ANITA BEER CO.
Bottled by Gutsch Brewing Co. Inc.
Label CA. U-Permit

LOS ANGELES – GUTSCH'S BREWING CO. INC.
Formerly X. L. Brewing Co. Inc.
1935 – 1937
Bottle Label CA. U-Permit

IRTP

LOS ANGELES – HOME BREWING CO.
AKA Imperial Brewing Co.
1933 – 1934
Label CA. U -Permit

LOS ANGELES – LOS ANGELES BREWING CO.
AKA Eastside Brewing Co.
Labels on Four Corners Pre-Prohibition
Center Label L- Permit

LOS ANGELES – LOS ANGELES BREWING CO.
AKA Eastside Brewing Co.
Label Pre-Prohibition
1897 – 1920
1933 - 1953

IRTP

IRTP

Pre-Prohibition

Pre-Prohhibition

LOS ANGELES – LOS ANGELES BREWING CO.
AKA Eastside Brewing Co.
1897 – 1920
Label Pre-Prohibition
1933 - 1953

CA. U-Permit   Pre-Prohibition   IRTP   Prohibition

LOS ANGELES – LOS ANGELES BREWING CO.
AKA Eastside Brewing Co.
1897 – 1920
1933 - 1953
Both Labels Pre-Prohibition

IRTP

IRTP

LOS ANGELES – LOS ANGELES BREWING CO.
AKA Mission Brewing Co.
1933 - 1953

CA. U-Permit

Pre-Prohibition

IRTP

IRTP

LOS ANGELES - MAIER BREWING CO.
1907 – 1971
Top Labels Pre-Prohibition
Center Left Label Pre-Prohibition
Center Right Label CA. U-Permit
Bottom Label IRTP

LOS ANGELES - MAIER BREWING CO.
1907 – 1971
Both Labels Prohibition

LOS ANGELES - MAIER BREWING CO.
1907 – 1971
Label CA. U-Permit

IRTP

IRTP

IRTP

IRTP

LOS ANGELES - MAIER BREWING CO.
1907 – 1971
Label IRTP

Prohibition

CA. U-Permit

CA. U-Permit

LOS ANGELES - MAIER BREWING CO.
1907 – 1971
Top Label IRTP
Bottom Label Prohibition

Pre-Prohibition　　　　　　　　　　　　　　　　**Pre-Prohibition**

LOS ANGELES - MAIER BREWING CO.
1907 – 1971
Bottled for O-MY BOTTLING CO.
Top Label L-19 permit
Bottom Label CA. U-Permit

LOS ANGELES – MATHIE BREWING CO.
1903 - 1920
All Labels Pre-Prohibition

LOS ANGELES – MONARCH BREWING CO.
1937 - 1941

IRTP

IRTP

IRTP

IRTP

LOS ANGELES – MONARCH BREWING CO.
1937 - 1941
Top Left Label CA. U-Permit
Other Labels IRTP

LOS ANGELES – MONARCH BREWING CO.
1937 - 1941
Labels IRTP

LOS ANGELES – MONTEREY BREWING CO.
1934 - 1937
Labels IRTP

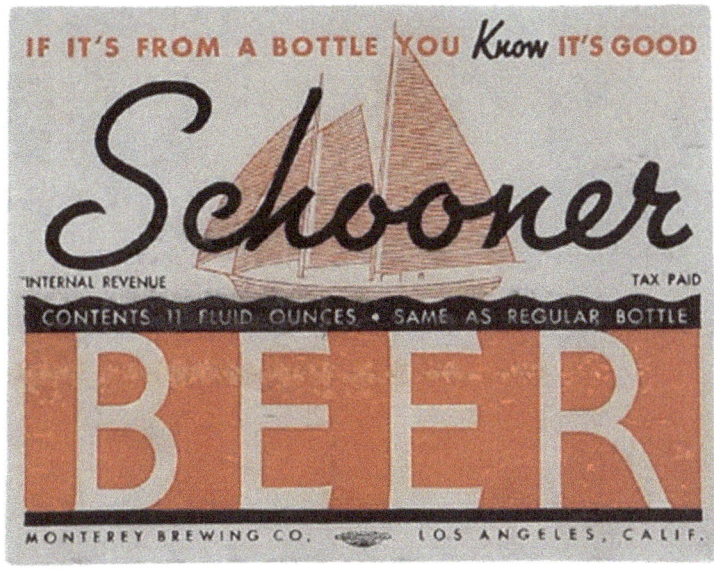

LOS ANGELES – RIO BREWING CO.
Labels CA. U-Permit

CA. U-Permit

LOS ANGELES – ROLLINSON BREWERY
Charles W. Rollinson
1937 - 1939
Labels IRTP

LOS ANGELES – SOUTHERN BREWERY
1951 – 1956
Labels IRTP

IRTP

LOS ANGELES - VERNON BREWING CO.
1933 - 1942
Label IRTP

IRTP   **IRTP**   **IRTP**   **CA. U-Permit**

LOS ANGELES - VERNON BREWING CO.
1933 – 1942
Top Left Label CA. U-Permit
Other Labels IRTP

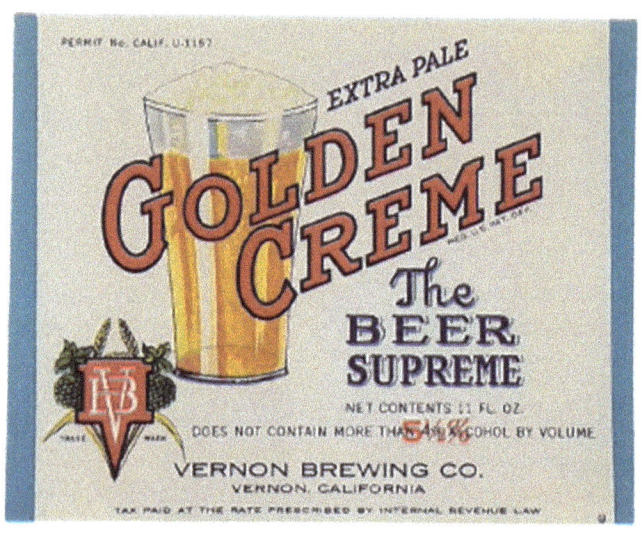

LOS ANGELES - VERNON BREWING CO.
1933 - 1942
Top Left Label CA. U-Permit
Other Labels IRTP

LOS ANGELES – WEST COAST BREWERIES
1933 - 1937
Labels CA. U-Permit

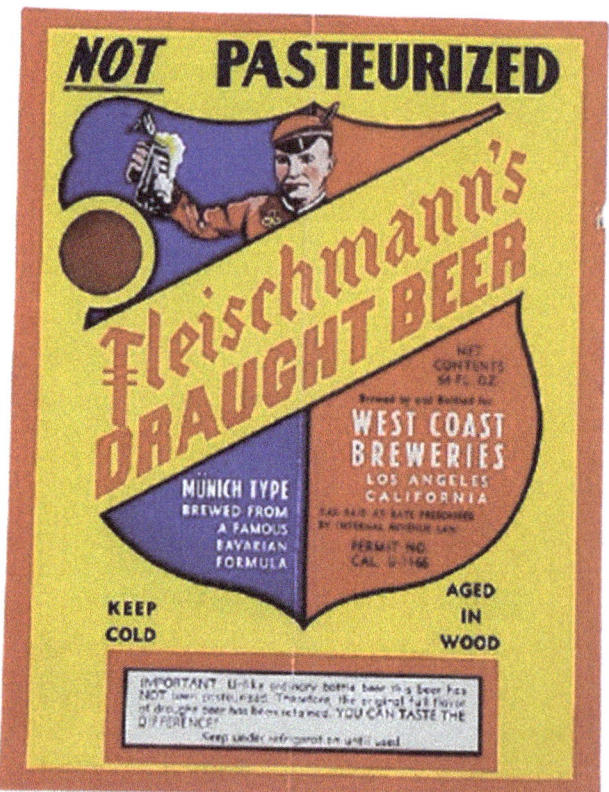

LOS ANGELES – WEST COAST BREWERIES
1933 – 1937
Top Left Label IRTP
Other Labels CA. U-Permit

LYNWOOD – LYNWOOD BREWING CO.
1934 - 1937
Labels CA. U-Permit

CA. U-Permit

CA. U-Permit

MODESTO, CA. – MODESTO BREWERY
1934 - 1938
Label IRTP

CA. U-Permit

CA. U-Permit

IRTP

CA. U-Permit

MODESTO. – MODESTO BREWERY
1934 - 1938
Labels IRTP

CA. U-Permit

CA. U-Permit

NAPA – CALIFORNIA BREWING ASSOCIATION
1907 - 1909
Labels Pre-Prohibition

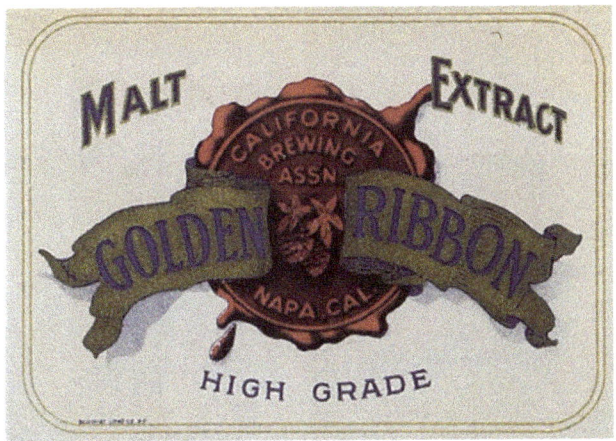

OAKLAND - OAKLAND BREWING & MALTING CO.
1907 – 1920
Label & Bottles Pre-Prohibition

Pre-Prohibition

Pre-Prohibition

Pre-Prohibition

Pre-Prohibition

OAKLAND - OAKLAND BREWING & MALTING CO.
1907 – 1920
Top Right Label IRTP
Other Labels Pre-Prohibition

OAKLAND – GOLDEN WEST BREWING CO.
1910 – 1915 West Berkeley
1911 – 1920 Oakland – 7th & Kirkham Sts.
1933 – 1950 Oakland – 533 Kirkham St.
Label Pre-Prohibition

Pre-Prohibition

Pre-Prohibition

Pre-Prohibition

Pre-Prohibition

Pre-Prohibition

OAKLAND – GOLDEN WEST BREWING CO.
1910 – 1915 West Berkeley
1911 – 1920 Oakland – 7th & Kirkham Sts.
1933 – 1950 Oakland – 533 Kirkham St.
Label IRTP

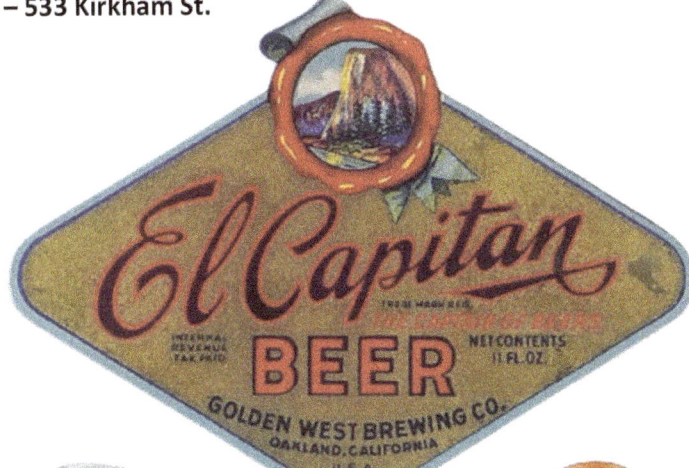

CA. U-Permit

CA. U-Permit

CA. U-Permit

CA. U-Permit

CA. U-Permit

OAKLAND – GOLDEN WEST BREWING CO.
1910 – 1915 West Berkeley
1911 – 1920 Oakland – 7th & Kirkham Sts.
1933 – 1950 Oakland – 533 Kirkham St.
Label IRTP

Quart Bottle
CA. U-Permit

CA. U-Permit

CA. U-Permit

Quart Bottle
CA. U-Permit

OAKLAND – GOLDEN WEST BREWING CO.
1910 – 1915 West Berkeley
1911 – 1920 Oakland – 7th & Kirkham Sts.
1933 – 1950 Oakland – 533 Kirkham St.
Label IRTP

CA. U-Permit

CA. U-Permit

IRTP

CA. U-Permit

IRTP

OAKLAND – GOLDEN WEST BREWING CO.
1910 – 1915 West Berkeley
1911 – 1920 Oakland – 7th & Kirkham Sts.
1933 – 1950 Oakland – 533 Kirkham St.
Label IRTP
Tonic Bottle L-Permit

L-Permit

IRTP

IRTP

IRTP

OAKLAND – GOLDEN WEST BREWING CO.
1910 – 1915 West Berkeley
1911 – 1920 Oakland – 7th & Kirkham Sts.
1933 – 1950 Oakland – 533 Kirkham St.
Label IRTP

IRTP

CA. U-Permit

Quart Bottle CA. U-Permit

CA. U-Permit

IRTP

OAKLAND – GOLDEN WEST BREWING CO.
1910 – 1915 West Berkeley
1911 – 1920 Oakland – 7th & Kirkham Sts.
1933 – 1950 Oakland – 533 Kirkham St.

IRTP

IRTP

CA. U-Permit

IRTP

IRTP

IRTP

OAKLAND – GOLDEN WEST BREWING CO.
1910 – 1915 West Berkeley
1911 – 1920 Oakland – 7th & Kirkham Sts.
1933 – 1950 Oakland – 533 Kirkham St.
Labels on left Side CA. U-Permit
Labels on Right Side IRTP

OAKLAND – GOLDEN WEST BREWING CO.
1910 – 1915 West Berkeley
1911 – 1920 Oakland – 7th & Kirkham Sts.
1933 – 1950 Oakland – 533 Kirkham St.
Top Label IRTP
Center & Bottom Labels L-12 Permit

OAKLAND - WUNDER BREWING CO.
1934 – 1934 NP
Top Label IRTP
Bottom Advertising Sign

OAKLAND - WUNDER BREWING CO.
1934 – 1934 NP
Top Label IRTP
Bottom Left Label CA. U-Permit
Bottom Right Label Prohibition

OAKLAND – SHASTA BRAND BEER
YOSEMITE COMPANY INC. SOLE DISTRIBUTORS
Label Pre-Prohibition

OXNARD – BOTTLED FOR CHARLES PEVERLEY
Label IRTP

RED BLUFF – RED BLUFF BREWING CO.
1937 - 1940
Labels IRTP

RED BLUFF – UNITED STATES BREWING CORP.
1942 - 1948
Labels IRTP

IRTP   IRTP   IRTP   IRTP

RED BLUFF – UNITED STATES BREWING CORP.
1942 - 1948
Labels IRTP

IRTP

IRTP

IRTP

IRTP

RED BLUFF – UNITED STATES BREWING CORP.
1942 - 1948
Labels IRTP

IRTP

IRTP

IRTP

IRTP

ROSEMEAD – IMPERIAL BREWING CO.
1934 - 1937
Labels CA. U-Permit

ROSEMEAD – OLDE TYME BREWING CORPORATION
1937 - 1937
Top Label CA. U-Permit
Other Labels IRTP

SACRAMENTO - BUFFALO BREWING CO.
1890 – 1897
BUFFALO BREWING CO. Branch of Sacramento Brewing Co.
1897 – 1920
Labels Pre-Prohibition

Pre-Prohibition

Pre-Prohibition

Center bottle Buffalo's first label
Pre-Prohibition

Pre-Prohibition

Pre-Prohibition

SACRAMENTO – CITY BREWERY - FRANK RUTHSTALLER – Branch of Sacramento Brewing Co.
1887 – 1897
SACRAMENTO – SACRAMENTO BREWING CO. – RUTHSTALLER BREWERY
1915 Label Pre-Prohibition

Pre-Pro

CA. U-Permit

Pre-Pro

Pre-Pro

Pre- Pro

SACRAMENTO - BUFFALO BREWING CO.
BUFFALO BREWING CO. Branch of Sacramento Brewing Co.
1890 – 1897
Label Pre-Prohibition

Pre-Prohibition

Pre-Prohibition

Pre-Prohibition

Pre-Prohibition

SACRAMENTO - BUFFALO BREWING CO.
BUFFALO BREWING CO. Branch of Sacramento Brewing Co.
1890 – 1942
Label CA. U-Permit

Pre-Prohibition

Pre-Prohibition

Prohibition

Prohibition

Prohibition

SACRAMENTO - BUFFALO BREWING CO.
BUFFALO BREWING CO. Branch of Sacramento Brewing Co.
1890 – 1942
Label CA. U-Permit

CA. U-Permit

Pre-Prohibition   Pre-Prohibition   Pre-Prohibition

IRTP

SACRAMENTO - BUFFALO BREWING CO.
BUFFALO BREWING CO. Branch of Sacramento Brewing Co.
1890 – 1942
Label IRTP

Pre-Prohibition

Pre-Prohibition

Pre-Prohibition

Pre-Prohibition

IRTP

SACRAMENTO - BUFFALO BREWING CO.
BUFFALO BREWING CO. Branch of Sacramento Brewing Co.
1890 – 1942
Top Left Label CA. U-Permit
Other Labels IRTP

SACRAMENTO - BUFFALO BREWING CO.
BUFFALO BREWING CO. - Branch of Sacramento Brewing Co.
1897 - 1920
1934 - 1942
Label IRTP

CA. U-Permit

IRTP

IRTP

IRTP

SACRAMENTO - BUFFALO BREWING CO.
BUFFALO BREWING CO.
Branch of Sacramento Brewing Co.
1897 - 1920
1934 - 1942
Labels IRTP

SACRAMENTO – GRACE BROS. INC. (Joseph T. Grace)
1942 – 1949
Labels IRTP

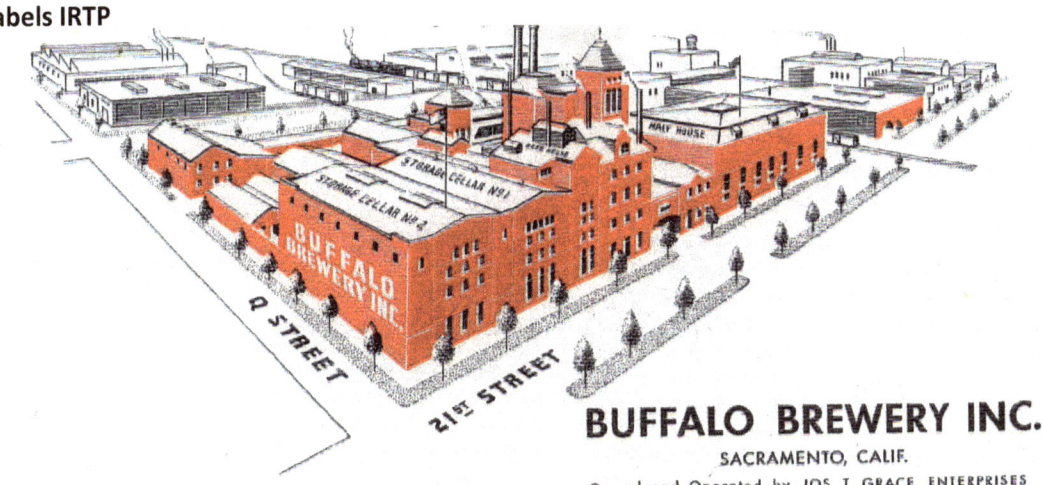

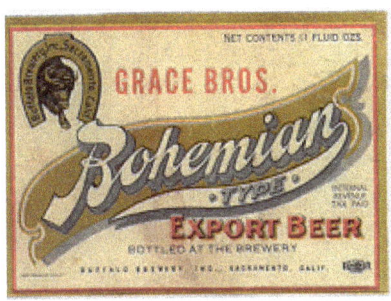  

SACRAMENTO – CAPITOL BREWING CO.
1933 – 1934
Alhambra Boulevard & C Street
Label CA. U-Permit

SACRAMENTO – STANDARD BREWING CORPORATION
1937 - 1937

IRTP

IRTP

IRTP

SALINAS – SALINAS BREWING CO.
1904 -1920
All Pre-Prohibition

Pre-Prohibition

SALINAS – SALINAS BREWING & ICE CO.
1934 - 1938
Top Label IRTP
Bottom Label CA. U-Permit

CA. U-Permit

CA. U-Permit

SALINAS – SALINAS BREWING & ICE CO.
1934 - 1938
Labels IRTP

SALINAS – SALINAS BREWING & ICE COMPANY
1934 – 1938
Top Label CA. U-Permit
Bottom Label IRTP

SALINAS - MONTEREY BREWING Co.
1938 – 1942
Top Label IRTP
Bottom Label CA. U-Permit

IRTP

IRTP

SALINAS - MONTEREY BREWING Co.
1938 – 1942
Label IRTP

IRTP   IRTP   IRTP   IRTP

SALINAS – MONTEREY BREWING CO.
1933 - 1948
Label IRTP

IRTP

IRTP   IRTP   IRTP

SAN DIEGO – AZTEC BREWING CO.
1933 - 1948
Top Label CA. U-Permit
Bottom Label IRTP

SAN DIEGO – AZTEC BREWING CO.
1933 - 1948
Label IRTP

IRTP

CA. U-Permit

IRTP

IRTP

CA. U-Permit

SAN DIEGO – AZTEC BREWING CO.
1933 - 1948
Label IRTP

IRTP

Painted Label
IRTP

IRTP

Painted Label
IRTP

IRTP

SAN DIEGO – AZTEC BREWING CO.
1933 - 1948
Labels IRTP

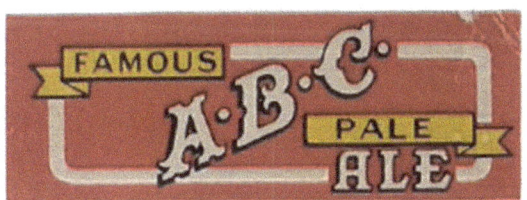

SAN DIEGO – AZTEC BREWING CO.
1933 - 1948
Labels CA. U-Permit

SAN DIEGO – AZTEC BREWING CO.
1933 - 1948
Top Label CA. U-Permit
Center & Bottom Labels IRTP

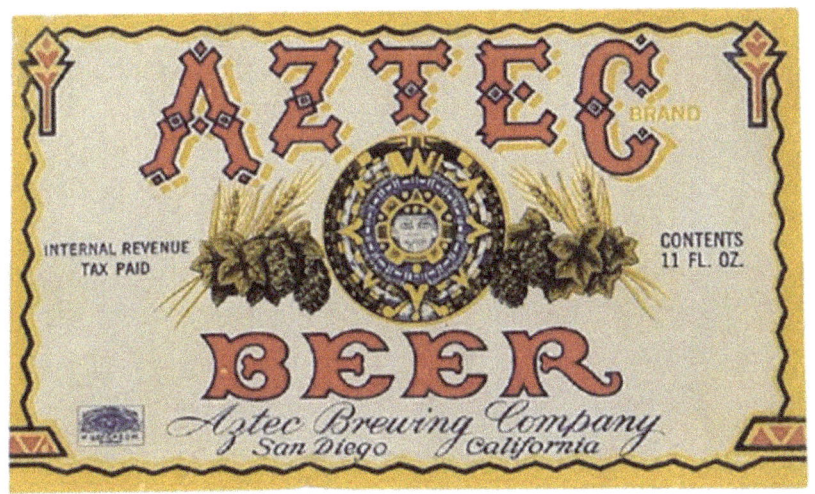

SAN DIEGO – AZTEC BREWING CO.
1933 - 1948
Labels IRTP

SAN DIEGO – AZTEC BREWING CO.
1933 - 1948
Labels IRTP

SAN DIEGO – AZTEC BREWING CO.
1933 - 1948
Labels IRTP

SAN DIEGO – AZTEC BREWING CO.
1933 - 1948
Labels IRTP

SAN DIEGO – SAN DIEGO BREWING CO.
1936 - 1942
Labels IRTP

IRTP

SAN DIEGO – BALBOA BREWING CO.
1933 - 1934
Label CA. U-Permit

SAN DIEGO – MISSION BREWING CO.
1912 – 1916
Label Pre-Prohibition

SAN FRANCISCO – ACME BREWING CO.
1907 – 1916
1401 Sansome & Greenwich Streets
Labels Pre-Prohibition

SAN FRANCISCO – ACME BREWING CO.
1907 – 1916
1401 Sansome & Greenwich Streets
Label Pre-Prohibition

Prohibition

Pre-Prohibition

Pre-Prohibition

Pre-Prohibition

SAN FRANCISCO – ACME BREWING CO.
1907 – 1916
1401 Sansome & Greenwich Streets
Top Label Prohibition
Bottom Label Pre-Prohibition

SAN FRANCISCO – ACME BREWING CO.
1907 – 1916
1401 Sansome & Greenwich Streets
Top & Center Labels Prohibition
Bottom Labels Pre-Prohibition

SAN FRANCISCO - ACME BREWERIES
1916 – 1920 (California Brewing Association)
1936 – 1943 (California Brewing Association)
Label Prohibition Non- Intoxicating

Prohibition

Prohibition

IRTP

IRTP

IRTP

SAN FRANCISCO - ACME BREWERIES
1916 – 1920 (California Brewing & Bottling Association)
1936 – 1943 (California Brewing & Bottling Association)
Label Pre-Prohibition

IRTP   IRTP   IRTP   Pre-Prohibition   CA. U-Permit   IRTP

SAN FRANCISCO – ACME BREWING CO.
1907 – 1916
1401 Sansome & Greenwich Streets
California Brewing Association
Top & Center Labels Prohibition
Bottom Label CA.U-Permit

SAN FRANCISCO - ACME BREWERIES
1916 – 1920 (California Brewing & Bottling Association)
1936 – 1943 (California Brewing & Bottling Association)
Labels Prohibition

SAN FRANCISCO – ACME BREWING CO.
1907 – 1916
1401 Sansome & Greenwich Streets
Top Left Label California Brewing Association Prohibition
Top Right Label Cereal Products Refining Corp. IRTP
Center & Bottom Labels IRTP

SAN FRANCISCO - ACME BREWERIES
1916 – 1920 (California Brewing & Bottling Association)
1936 – 1943 (California Brewing & Bottling Association)
Labels Prohibition
Neck Labels Mixture Pre-Prohibition & Prohibition

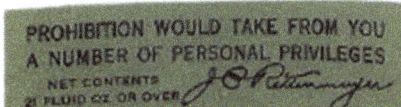

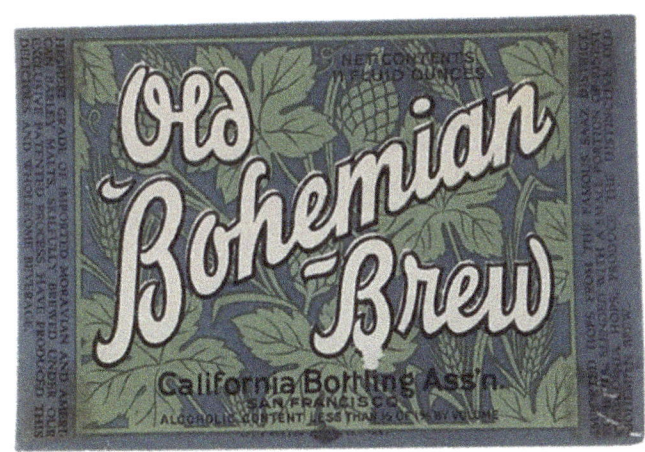

SAN FRANCISCO - ACME BREWERIES
1916 – 1920 (California Brewing & Bottling Association)
1936 – 1943 (California Brewing & Bottling Association)
Label Pre-Prohibition

Pre-Prohibition

Pre-Prohibition

CA. U-Permit

CA. U-Permit

SAN FRANCISCO - ACME BREWERIES
1916 – 1920 (California Brewing & Bottling Association)
1936 – 1943 (California Brewing & Bottling Association)
Label Prohibition

IRTP　　　　　　　　　　　　　　　　　　　　　　　　　　　　　　IRTP

　　　　　　　　　　IRTP　　　　　　IRTP

SAN FRANCISCO - ACME BREWERIES
1936 – 1943 (California Brewing & Bottling Association)
Label IRTP

IRTP

IRTP

IRTP   IRTP

SAN FRANCISCO - ACME BREWERIES
1916 – 1920 (California Brewing & Bottling Association)
1936 – 1943 (California Brewing & Bottling Association)
Label Prohibition 1% CA. H 10520 Permit

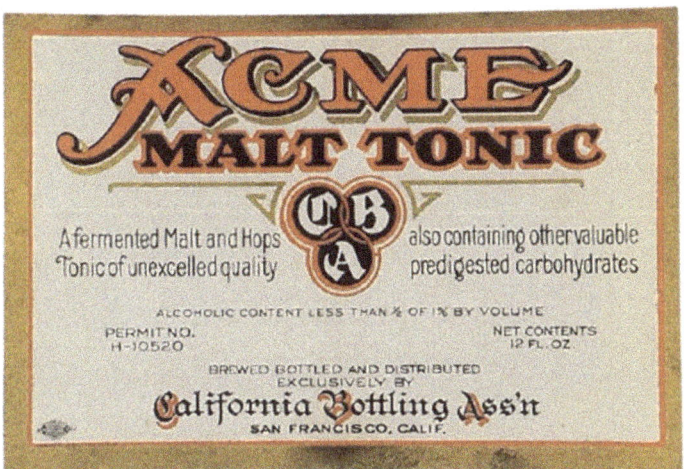

Prohibition

Prohibition

Prohibition

SAN FRANCISCO - ALBANY BREWERY
HAGEMANN BREWING CO.
1882 - 1888
Label Pre-Prohibition
Both Labels on Two Center Bottles Applied

Pre-Prohibition

Pre-Prohibition

Pre-Prohibition

Pre-Prohibition

SAN FRANCISCO - ALBION BREWING INC.
1911 -1920
1937 - 1941
Label IRTP

IRTP

IRTP

IRTP

IRTP

SAN FRANCISCO - ALBION BREWING INC.
1911 -1920
1937 - 1941
Label IRTP

IRTP

IRTP

IRTP

IRTP

IRTP

SAN FRANCISCO - ALBION BREWING INC.
1911 -1920
1937 - 1941
Labels IRTP

SAN FRANCISCO - ALBION BREWING INC.
1911 -1920
1937 - 1941
Labels IRTP

SAN FRANCISCO - ALBION BREWING INC.
1911 -1920
1937 - 1941
Labels IRTP

SAN FRANCISCO - ANCHOR BREWING CO.
1895 – 1906
1906 – To Date
Label CA. U-Permit

SAN FRANCISCO OAKLAND – APPLEDORN'S BREWING CO.
Pre- Prohibition
Special Brew NA
Label Prohibition

SAN FRANCISCO – BAVARIAN BREWERY
1897 – 1898
John Kroger Advertisement Pre-Prohibition
Label Pre-Prohibition
919 Capp Street

Pre-Prohibition

SAN FRANCISCO – BLUE & GOLD BREWING CO.
Label Pre-Prohibition

Pre-Prohibition

SAN FRANCISCO - EAGLE BREWING CO.
1901 – 1911
Label IRTP

CA. U-Permit

CA. U- Permit

CA. U-Permit

CA. U-Permit

SAN FRANCISCO - EAGLE BREWING CO.
1901 – 1911
Labels IRTP

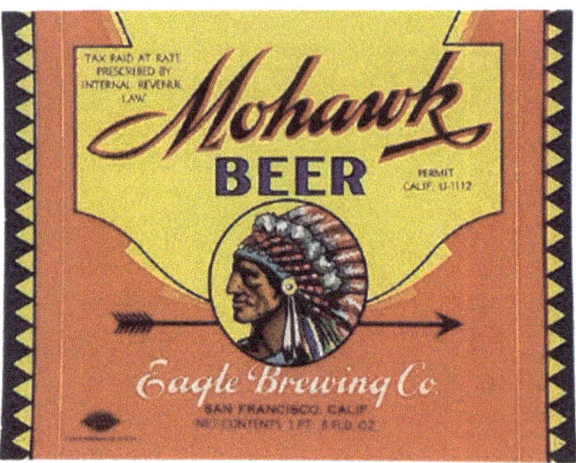

IRTP

IRTP

IRTP

SAN FRANCISCO - EL REY BREWING CO.
1933 – 1937
Label IRTP

CA. U-Permit

CA. U-Permit

IRTP

IRTP

IRTP

SAN FRANCISCO - EL REY BREWING CO.
1933 - 1937
Top Left Label IRTP
Other Labels CA. U-Permit

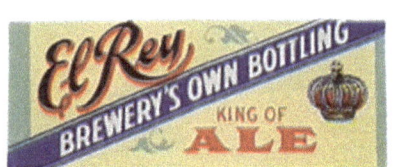

SAN FRANCISCO - EL REY BREWING CO.
1933 - 1937
Labels IRTP

SAN FRANCISCO - EL REY BREWING CO.
1933 - 1937
Labels IRTP

SAN FRANCISCO - CONSUMERS BREWING & BOTTLING CO. (El Rey Brewer)
Pre-Prohibition
Labels IRTP

SAN FRANCISCO - CONSUMERS BREWING & BOTTLING CO. (El Rey Brewer)
Top Label Pre-Prohibition
Bottom Keg Label IRTP

SAN FRANCISCO – ENTERPRISE - PIONEER BOTTLING CO.
El Rey Brewing Co.
1933 - 1937
Label CA. U-Permit

SAN FRANCISCO - ENTERPRISE BOTTLING CO.
1892 – 1914
1914 – 1920
Label Pre-Prohibition

SAN FRANCISCO - ENTERPRISE BOTTLING CO.
1892 – 1914
1914 – 1920
Labels Pre-Prohibition

SAN FRANCISCO - ENTERPRISE BOTTLING CO.
1892 – 1914
1914 – 1920

Pre-Prohibition   Pre-Prohibition   Pre-Prohibition   Pre-Prohibition

SAN FRANCISCO - GENERAL BREWING CORPORATION
1934 – 1948
LUCKY LAGER BREWING CO.
1948 – 1963
Labels CA. U-Permit

SAN FRANCISCO - GENERAL BREWING CORPORATION
1934 – 1948
LUCKY LAGER BREWING CO.
1948 – 1963
Labels CA. U-Permit

CA. U-Permit

CA. U-Permit

IRTP

IRTP

IRTP

SAN FRANCISCO - GENERAL BREWING CORPORATION
1934 – 1948
LUCKY LAGER BREWING CO.
1948 - 1963
Label IRTP

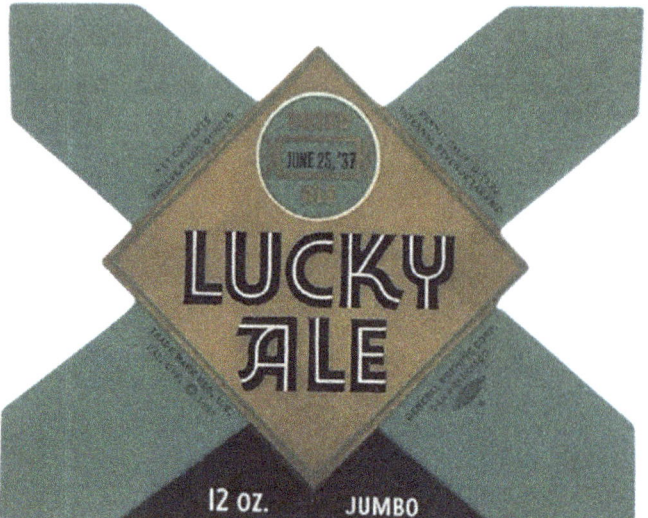

CA. U-Permit

IRTP

IRTP

CA. U-Permit

CA. U-Permit

SAN FRANCISCO - GENERAL BREWING CORPORATION
1934 – 1948
LUCKY LAGER BREWING CO.
1948 - 1963
Top Labels CA. U-Permit
Bottom Labels IRTP

SAN FRANCISCO - GENERAL BREWING CORPORATION
1934 – 1948
LUCKY LAGER BREWING CO.
1948 - 1963

All Bottles IRTP

SAN FRANCISCO - GLOBE BREWING CO.
1933- 1938
Label IRTP

IRTP

IRTP

IRTP

IRTP

IRTP

150

SAN FRANCISCO - GLOBE BREWING CO.
1933- 1938
Labels CA. U-Permit

SAN FRANCISCO - GLOBE BREWING CO.
1933- 1938
Labels IRTP

SAN FRANCISCO - GLOBE BREWING CO.
Bottled For Golden Ribbon Bottling Co.
1933- 1938

CA. U-Permit CA. U-Permit

SAN FRANCISCO - HAGEMANN BREWING CO.
1900 – 1920
Labels Pre-Prohibition
Golden Gate Steam Beer temporary label CA. Permit U-1155
(See Albany Brewery)

SAN FRANCISCO - JACKSON BREWING CO.
1874 – 1920
Labels Pre-Prohibition
1934 – 1934 NP

SAN FRANCISCO - JAPAN BREWING CO.
Masa Mune
C. 1904
Label Pre-Prohibition

SAN FRANCISCO – AUGUST LANG & CO.
1908- 1911
August Lang Brewing Association
1911 - 1912
Label Pre-Prohibition

Pre-Prohibition

SAN FRANCISCO - MAVERICKS
Label Export for W. R. Grace & Co.
No connection to Grace Bros.
William Randolph Grace had offices in Peru, Chile and Argentina
He owned a Steamship Company. Beer probably sold on his ships.

CITY BREW
Bottled By City Bottling Works
Bottle Pre-Prohibition

OLYMPUS LAGER BEER
Bottled By MOLAKIDIS BROS.
Label & Bottle Pre-Prohibition

OLD SAXON BEER
Especially Brewed For
OLD SAXON PRODUCTS CO.
Bottle IRTP

Pre-Prohibition

Pre-Prohibition

IRTP

SAN FRANCISCO - MILWAUKEE BREWERY OF SAN FRANCISCO
1895 – 1902
1902 – 1920
1933 - 1935
Top Label Prohibition CA. Permit H-10500
Bottle Label Prohibition

Pre-Prohibition

SAN FRANCISCO - MILWAUKEE BREWERY OF SAN FRANCISCO
Brewed and Bottled for Astor Wine Company
1895 – 1902
1902 – 1920
1933 - 1935
Label Pre-Prohibition

SAN FRANCISCO - MILWAUKEE BREWERY OF SAN FRANCISCO
Bottled for Denver Bottling Co.
1041 Sansome Street
1895 – 1902
1902 – 1920
1933 - 1935
Label Pre-Prohibition

SAN FRANCISCO - MILWAUKEE BREWERY OF SAN FRANCISCO
Bottled By Liberty Bottling Co.
2455 Lombard Street
Label IRTP

SAN FRANCISCO - MILWAUKEE BREWERY OF SAN FRANCISCO
Brewed Expressly for John Fauser Co.
1895 – 1902
1902 – 1920
1933 - 1935
Label Pre-Prohibition

SAN FRANCISCO - MILWAUKEE BREWERY OF SAN FRANCISCO
Bottled By E. H. Schade
1327 Laguna Street
1895 – 1902
1902 – 1920
1933 - 1935
Labels Pre-Prohibition

Pre-Prohibition

Pre-Prohibition

SAN FRANCISCO - MILWAUKEE BREWERY OF SAN FRANCISCO
Bottled By E. H. Schade
1327 Laguna Street
1895 – 1902
1902 – 1920
1933 - 1935
Labels Pre-Prohibition

SAN FRANCISCO - MILWAUKEE BREWERY OF SAN FRANCISCO
1895 – 1902
1902 – 1920
1933 - 1935
Label CA. L-Permit

L-Permit   L-Permit   Pre-Prohibition   L-Permit   L-Permit

SAN FRANCISCO - MILWAUKEE BREWERY OF SAN FRANCISCO
1895 – 1902
1902 – 1920
1933 - 1935
Both Labels CA. U-Permit

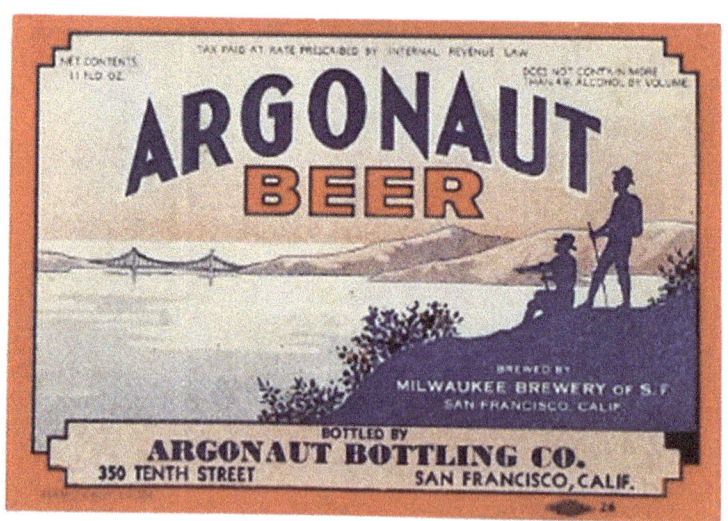

SAN FRANCISCO - MILWAUKEE BREWERY OF SAN FRANCISCO
1895 – 1902
1902 – 1920
1933 - 1935
Label CA. U-Permit

CA. U-Permit

CA, U-Permit

CA. U-Permit

CA. U-Permit

CA. U-Permit

SAN FRANCISCO - MILWAUKEE BREWERY OF SAN FRANCISCO
1895 – 1902
1902 – 1920
1933 - 1935
Top Label IRTP
Bottom Label CA. U-Permit

SAN FRANCISCO - MILWAUKEE BREWERY OF SAN FRANCISCO
1895 – 1902
1902 – 1920
1933 - 1935
Top Label CA. L-Permit
Bottom Label Prohibition

SAN FRANCISCO - MILWAUKEE BREWERY OF SAN FRANCISCO
DBA GARDEN CITY BREWERY SAN JOSE
1906 - 1920
Both Labels CA. U-Permit

SAN FRANCISCO – NATIONAL BREWING CO.
1884 – 1916
722 Fulton & Webster Streets
Labels Pre-Prohibition

SAN FRANCISCO – NATIONAL BOTTLING WORKS
Corner Fulton & Webster Streets
1884 - 1916
Labels Pre-Prohibition

Pre-Prohibition   **Pre-Prohibition**   **Pre-Prohibition**

SAN FRANCISCO – NATIONAL BOTTLING WORKS
1884 – 1916
722 Fulton & Webster Streets
Both Labels Pre-Prohibition

SAN FRANCISCO – NATIONAL BOTTLING WORKS
1884 – 1916
564 Fulton & Webster Streets
1565 Linden Street, Oakland
Both Labels Pre-Prohibition

SAN FRANCISCO – NATIONAL BREWING CO.
1884 – 1916
564 Fulton & Webster Streets
Label Export Tax Free Pre-Prohibition

Pre-Prohibition

Pre-Prohibition

Pre-Prohibition

SAN FRANCISCO – NORTH STAR BREWERY
1897 - 1920
1934 – 1935
Labels IRTP

IRTP

SAN FRANCISCO – NORTH STAR BREWERY
1897 - 1920
1934 – 1935
Top Label IRTP

SAN FRANCISCO – OLD DUTCH BREW CO.
Brewed And Bottled for Old Dutch Brew Company
San Francisco California, U.S.A.
Label Pre-Prohibition

SAN FRANCISCO – OLD LAGER BREWING CO.
AKA OLD GERMAN LAGER BREWING CO.
Label Pre-Prohibition

Pre-Prohibition   Pre-Prohibition

SAN FRANCISCO – OLYMPIA BOTTLING CO.
1423 Sansome Street
1916
Label & Bottle Pre-Prohibition

Pre-Prohibition

SAN FRANCISCO – PACIFIC BREWING & MALTING CO.
1914 – 1920
San Francisco – Oakland - Sacramento
Label CA. U-Permit

SAN FRANCISCO - PHOENIX BOTTLING WORKS
1877 – 1904
Thomas J. Kirby
1904 – 1906
Estate of Thomas J. Kirby
528 Noe Street
John Fauser & Company
Guerrero Street
Top Label IRTP
Bottom Label Pre-Prohibition

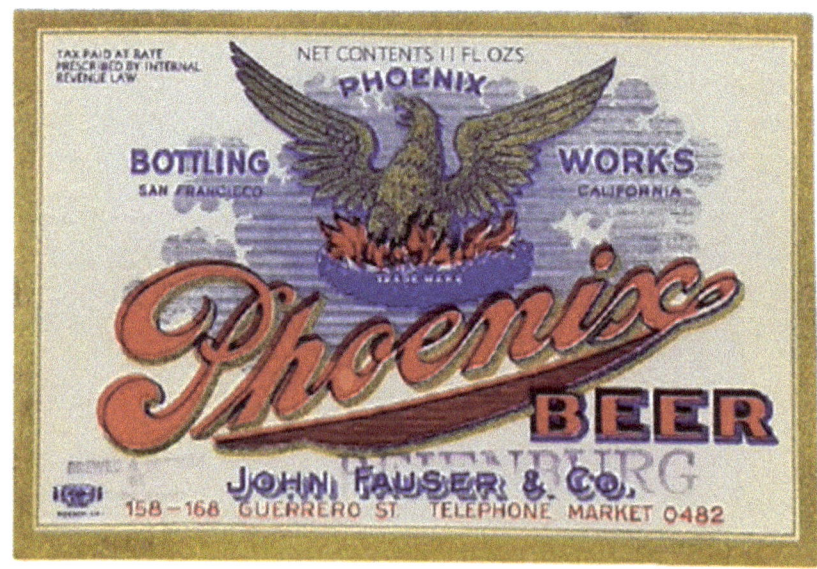

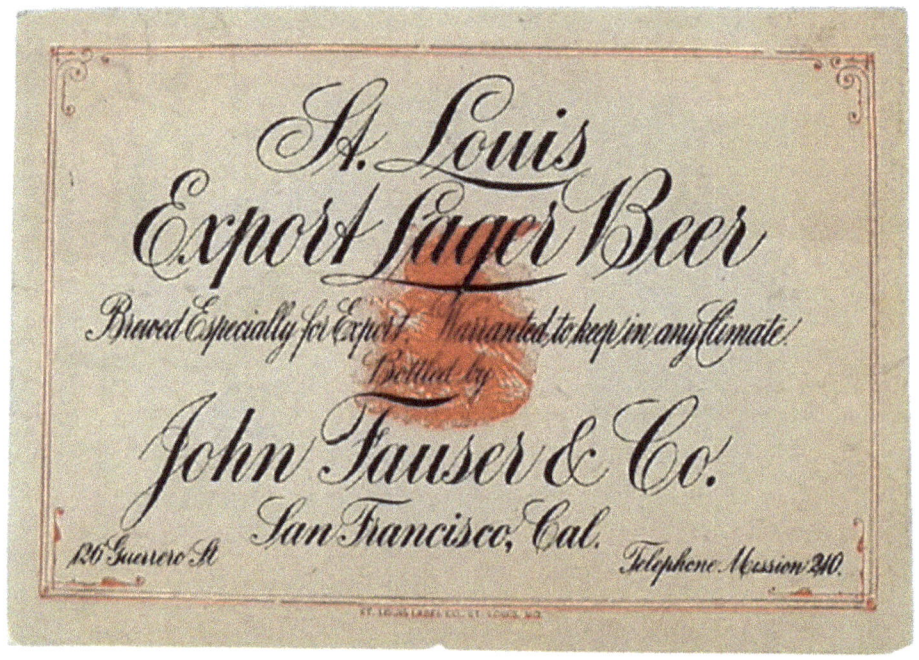

SAN FRANCISCO – SAN FRANCISCO BREWING CORPORATION
(General Enterprise Company)
Top Label IRTP
Bottom Label CA. L-4 Permit

SAN FRANCISCO – JOSEPH SCHWARTZ BREWING CO.
1904 – 1914
Both Labels Pre-Prohibition

Pre-Prohibition

Pre-Prohibition

SAN FRANCISCO – SUPREME HOME BREW
SUPREME BEVERAGE CO.
2251 Chestnut Street
Bottle & Label Prohibition

Prohibition

SAN FRANCISCO – HOP BREW BEER NA
Club Bottlers San Francisco
18 Natomas Street
Bottle & Label Prohibition Home Additive

Prohibition

SAN FRANCISO – UNITED STATES BREWERY & MALT
1884 – 1890
1890 – 1893
1893 – 1906
Label Pre-Prohibition

SAN FRANCISCO – VIKING BREWERY
1895 – 1897
Label Pre-Prohibition

SAN FRANCISCO – RAINIER BREWING CO.
1550 Bryant Street
Labels Prohibition

SAN FRANCISCO – RAINIER BREWING CO.
1550 Bryant Street
1915 – 1953
Label Pre-Prohibition

Pre-Prohibition

Pre-Prohibition

Prohibition

Pre-Prohibition

Pre-Prohibition

SAN FRANCISCO – RAINIER BREWING CO.
1550 Bryant Street
1915 - 1953
Label CA. U-Permit

CA. U-Permit

CA. U-Permit

Pre-Prohibition

Pre-Prohibition

Pre-Prohibition

SAN FRANCISCO – RAINIER BREWING CO.
1550 Bryant Street
1915 – 1953
Label Prohibition

CA. U-Permit

CA. U-Permit

Prohibition

Prohibition

Prohibition

SAN FRANCISCO – RAINIER BREWING CO.
1550 Bryant Street
1915 - 1953
Label CA. U-Permit

Prohibition

Pre-Prohibition

Pre-Prohibition

CA. U-Permit

CA. U-Permit

186

SAN FRANCISCO – RAINIER BREWING CO.
1550 Bryant Street
1915 - 1953
Label CA. U-Permit

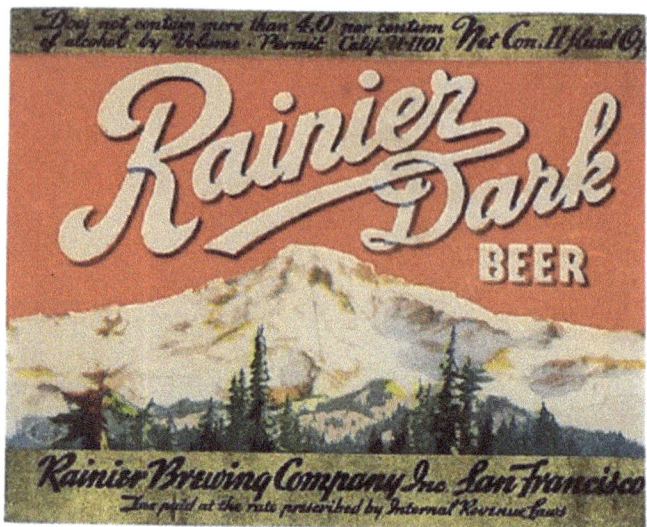

IRTP

CA. U-Permit

CA. U-Permit

SAN FRANCISCO – RAINIER BREWING CO.
1550 Bryant Street
1915 - 1953
Labels IRTP

IRTP

IRTP

SAN FRANCISCO – RAINIER BREWING CO.
1550 Bryant Street
1915 – 1953
Label IRTP

IRTP

IRTP

IRTP

IRTP

SAN FRANCISCO – RAINIER BREWING CO.
1550 Bryant Street
1915 – 1953

IRTP

IRTP

IRTP

IRTP

IRTP

IRTP

SAN FRANCISCO – RAINIER BREWING CO.
1550 Bryant Street
1915 – 1953
Label IRTP

IRTP

IRTP

IRTP

SAN FRANCISCO – RAINIER BREWING CO.
1550 Bryant Street
1915 – 1953
Label IRTP

IRTP

IRTP

IRTP

IRTP

IRTP

SAN FRANCISCO – RAINIER BREWING CO.
1550 Bryant Street
1915 – 1953
Top Label Prohibition
Bottom Left Label CA. U-Permit
Bottom Right Label Pre-Prohibition

CA. U-Permit

SAN FRANCISCO – RAINIER BREWING CO.
1550 Bryant Street
1915 – 1953
Labels IRTP

SAN FRANCISCO – RAINIER BREWING CO.
1550 Bryant Street
1915 - 1953
Top Left Label CA. U-Permit
Labels IRTP

SAN FRANCISCO – RAINIER BREWING CO.
1550 Bryant Street
1915 - 1953
Labels IRTP

SAN FRANCISCO – RAINIER BREWING CO.
1550 Bryant Street
1915 - 1953
Both Labels on Left Side CA. U-Permit
Label Top Right IRTP
Label Bottom Right Prohibition CA. H-10134 Permit

SAN FRANCISCO – RAINIER BREWING CO.
1550 Bryant Street
1915 - 1953
Schwartz Ginger Ale Company
Label CA. U-Permit

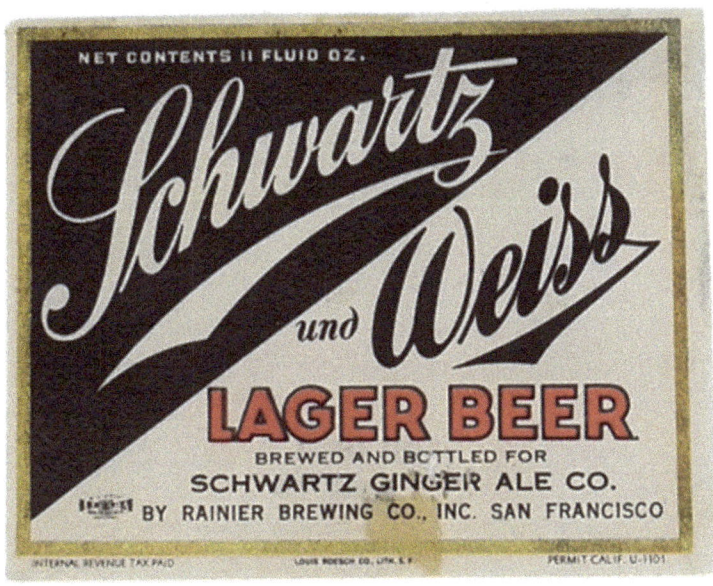

SAN FRANCISCO – RAINIER BREWING CO.
550 Bryant Street
1933 - 1953
L. H. Leidig
Label CA. U-Permit

SAN FRANCISCO – PACIFIC BREWING CO.
Pacific Products
1905 - 1953
Label IRTP

CA. U-Permit

Pre-Prohibition

CA. U-Permit

SAN FRANCISCO - TACOMA BREWERY
1550 Bryant Street
1905 - 1953
Label Prohibition

IRTP

IRTP

IRTP

IRTP

IRTP

SAN FRANCISCO – TACOMA BREWERY
1550 Bryant Street
1905 - 1953
Left Label Prohibition
Right Label IRTP
Tacoma Malt Bottle 1912

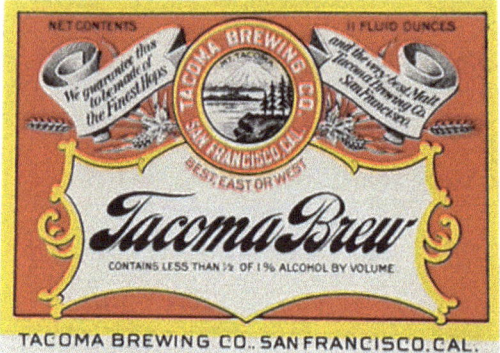

IRTP   Prohibition   Pre-Prohibition   Prohibition

SAN FRANCISCO – CONSUMERS & NORTH STAR BOTTLING WORKS
Pre-Prohibition
Carl A. Tornberg
1905 - 1913
Both Labels CA. U-Permit

SAN FRANCISCO – CONSUMERS & NORTH STAR BOTTLING WORKS
Pre-Prohibition
Carl A. Tornberg
1905 - 1913
Top Label CA. U-Permit
Bottom Label IRTP

SAN FRANCISCO - REGAL PRODUCTS CO.
1933 - 1935
3250 Twentieth Street
Labels IRTP

SAN FRANCISCO – REGAL AMBER BREWING CO.
1935 – 1950
Labels IRTP

SAN FRANCISCO – REGAL AMBER BREWING CO.
1935 – 1950
Label CA. U-Permit

CA. U-Permit

CA. U-Permit

CA. U-Permit

CA. U-Permit

CA. U-Permit

SAN FRANCISCO – REGAL AMBER BREWING CO.
1935 – 1950
Label IRTP

IRTP

IRTP

IRTP

IRTP

IRTP

SAN FRANCISCO – REGAL AMBER BREWING CO.
1935 – 1950
Label IRTP

CA. U-Permit

IRTP

IRTP

IRTP

IRTP

SAN FRANCISCO – REGAL AMBER BREWING CO.
1935 – 1950
Top Label IRTP
Bottom Labels U-Permit

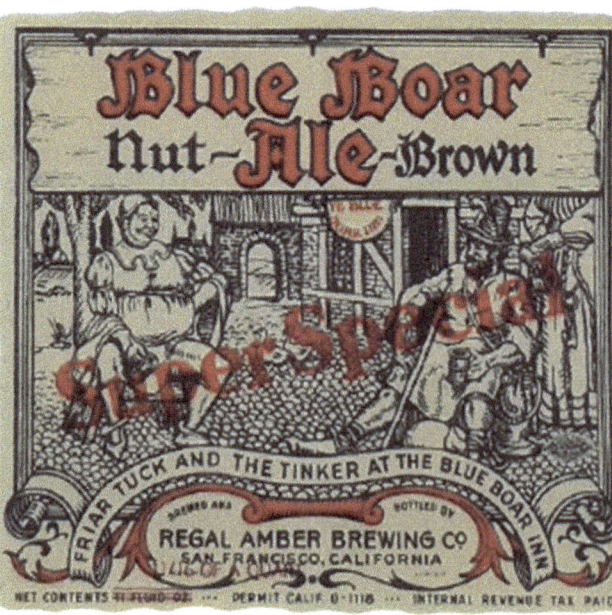

SAN FRANCISCO – REGAL AMBER BREWING CO.
1935 – 1950
Top & Center Labels IRTP
Bottom Label CA. U-Permit

SAN FRANCISCO – SAN FRANCISCO BREWING CORPORATION
Formerly Milwaukee Brewery San Francisco
Brewed and Bottled for Tornberg's Botting Co.
1935 - 1956
Labels IRTP

IRTP

SAN FRANCISCO – SAN FRANCISCO BREWING CORPORATION
Formerly Milwaukee Brewery San Francisco
1935 - 1956
Labels CA. U-Permit

CA. U-Permit

IRTP

SAN FRANCISCO – SAN FRANCISCO BREWING CORPORATION
Formerly Milwaukee Brewery San Francisco
1935 - 1956
Label IRTP

IRTP

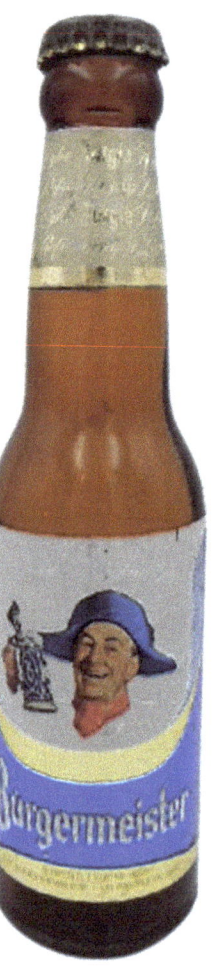

IRTP

IRTP

IRTP

IRTP

SAN FRANCISCO – SAN FRANCISCO BREWING CORPORATION
Formerly Milwaukee Brewery San Francisco
1935 - 1956
Label IRTP

IRTP

IRTP

IRTP

CA. U-Permit

CA. U-Permit

SAN FRANCISCO – SAN FRANCISCO BREWING CORPORATION
Formerly Milwaukee Brewery San Francisco
1935 - 1956
Label Withdrawn Free of Tax for Exportation

IRTP

IRTP   IRTP

IRTP

SAN FRANCISCO – SAN FRANCISCO BREWING CORPORATION
Formerly Milwaukee Brewery San Francisco
1935 - 1956
Labels IRTP

SAN FRANCISCO – SAN FRANCISCO BREWING CORPORATION
Formerly Milwaukee Brewery San Francisco
1935 - 1956
Label IRTP

IRTP

IRTP

IRTP

IRTP

IRTP

SAN FRANCISCO – SAN FRANCISCO BREWING CORPORATION
Formerly Milwaukee Brewery San Francisco
Brewed and Bottled Especially for General Enterprise Co.
1935 - 1956
Label IRTP

IRTP **IRTP** **IRTP** **IRTP**

SAN FRANCISCO – SAN FRANCISCO BREWING CORPORATION
Formerly Milwaukee Brewery San Francisco
Brewed and Bottled Especially for General Enterprise Co.
1935 - 1956
Labels IRTP

IRTP

IRTP

SAN FRANCISCO – SAN FRANCISCO BREWING CORPORATION
Formerly Milwaukee Brewery San Francisco
1935 - 1956
Label IRTP

IRTP

IRTP

IRTP

SAN FRANCISCO – SAN FRANCISCO BREWING CORPORATION
Formerly Milwaukee Brewery San Francisco
Distributed by Hibernia Brewing Co.
1935 - 1956
Labels IRTP

SAN FRANCISCO – SAN FRANCISCO BREWING CORPORATION
Formerly Milwaukee Brewery San Francisco
Brewed and Bottled for Golden Brand Bottling Co.
1935 - 1956
Labels IRTP

IRTP

SAN FRANCISCO – SAN FRANCISCO BREWING CORPORATION
Formerly Milwaukee Brewery San Francisco
Brewed and Bottled for Denver Bottling Co.
1935 - 1956
Label IRTP

SAN FRANCISCO – SAN FRANCISCO BREWING CORPORATION
Formerly Milwaukee Brewery San Francisco
Brewed and Bottled for L. H. Leidig Salinas, Calif.
1935 - 1956
Label IRTP

SAN FRANCISCO – SAN FRANCISCO BREWING CORPORATION
Formerly Milwaukee Brewery San Francisco
Brewed and Bottled for Rishwain Bros. Stockton
1935 - 1956
Top Labels IRTP

SAN FRANCISCO – SAN FRANCISCO BREWING CORPORATION
Formerly Milwaukee Brewery San Francisco
Brewed and Bottled for Milonas & Sons Inc. San Francisco
1935 - 1956
Label IRTP

SAN FRANCISCO – SAN FRANCISCO BREWING CORPORATION
Formerly Milwaukee Brewery San Francisco
1935 - 1956
Top Labels IRTP

SAN FRANCISCO – SAN FRANCISCO BREWING CORPORATION
Formerly Milwaukee Brewery San Francisco
King's Taste Brewed for Hagstrom's Food Stores
Pioneer Beer brewed for Peer Brewing Co. Sacramento
1935 - 1956
Bottom Labels IRTP

SAN FRANCISCO – SAN FRANCISCO BREWING CORPORATION
Formerly Milwaukee Brewery San Francisco
Brewed and Bottled for Monterey Brewing Co. Salinas, Calif.
1935 - 1956
Top Labels IRTP

SAN FRANCISCO – SAN FRANCISCO BREWING CORPORATION
Formerly Milwaukee Brewery San Francisco
Brewed and Bottled for Globe Brewing Co. Los Angeles
1935 - 1956
Bottom Label IRTP

IRTP

SAN FRANCISCO – SAN FRANCISCO BREWING CORPORATION
Formerly Milwaukee Brewery San Francisco
Brewed and Bottled for Globe Brewing Co. Los Angeles
1935 - 1956
Labels IRTP

IRTP

IRTP

IRTP

SAN FRANCISCO – UNION BREWING & MALTING CO.
Brewed and Bottled for John K. Coburg
1902 – 1916
Label Pre-Prohibition

Pre-Prohibition

Pre-Prohibition

Pre-Prohibition

SAN FRANCISCO -UNION BREWING & MALTING CO.
1902 – 1916
Labels Pre-Prohibition

SAN FRANCISCO – UNION BREWING & MALTING CO.
1902 - 1916
Labels Pre-Prohibition

SAN FRANCISCO – UNION BREWING CO.
Top label Brewed and Bottled for N. Cervelli Bottling Co.
1902 - 1916
Labels Pre-Prohibition

Pre-Prohibition

SAN FRANCISCO – UNION BREWING CO.
1902 – 1916
Labels Pre-Prohibition

BOCA – BOCA BREWERY
1st California Lager Beer 1875

Pre-Prohibition

SAN FRANCISCO – JOHN WIELAND BREWERY
1856 – 1920
AKA California Brewing Co.
1932 – 1934 NP
Label Pre-Prohibition

Pre-Prohibition

Pre-Prohibition

Pre-Prohibition

Pre-Prohibition

Pre-Prohibition

SAN FRANCISCO – JOHN WIELAND BREWERY
1856 – 1920
Bottom Label Shows Brewed and Bottled for J. R. Luttrell & Son San Diego
1932 – 1934 NP
Top Label Prohibition
Bottom Label Pre-Prohibition

Pre-Prohibition

Pre-Prohibition

SAN FRANCISCO – JOHN WIELAND BREWERY
1856 – 1920
1932 – 1934 NP
1890 Label Pre-Prohibition Tax Free Export

Pre-Prohibition

Pre-Prohibition

Pre-Prohibition

SAN FRANCISCO – JOHN WIELAND BREWERY
1856 – 1920
1932 – 1934 NP
Labels Pre-Prohibition

SAN FRANCISCO – JOHN WIELAND BREWERY
1856 – 1920
Label Shows Brewed and Bottled for Yuba Bottling Works
1932 – 1934 NP
Label Pre-Prohibition

Pre-Prohibition

Pre-Prohibition

Pre-Prohibition

Pre-Prohibition

Pre-Prohibition

SAN FRANCISCO – JOHN WIELAND BREWERY
1856 – 1920
1932 – 1934 NP
Label Pre-Prohibition

Pre-Prohibition
N. Mugler

Pre-Prohibition
N. Mugler

Pre-Prohibition
Joe Souza

Pre-Prohibition
N. Mugler

Pre-Prohibition
N. Mugler

238

SAN FRANCISCO – JOHN WIELAND BREWERY
1856 – 1920
1932 – 1934 NP
Labels Pre-Prohibition

Pre-Prohibition

Pre-Prohibition

Pre-Prohibition

Pre-Prohibition

Prohibition

239

SAN FRANCISCO – JOHN WIELAND BREWERY
1856 – 1920
1932 – 1934 NP
Labels Prohibition

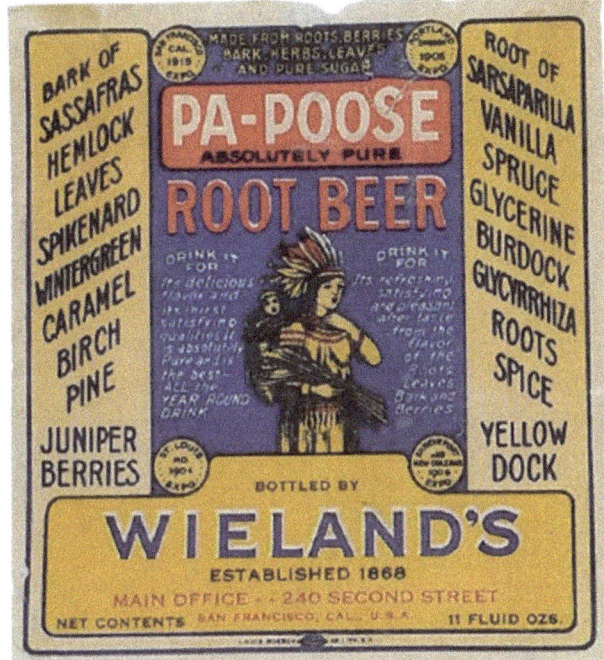

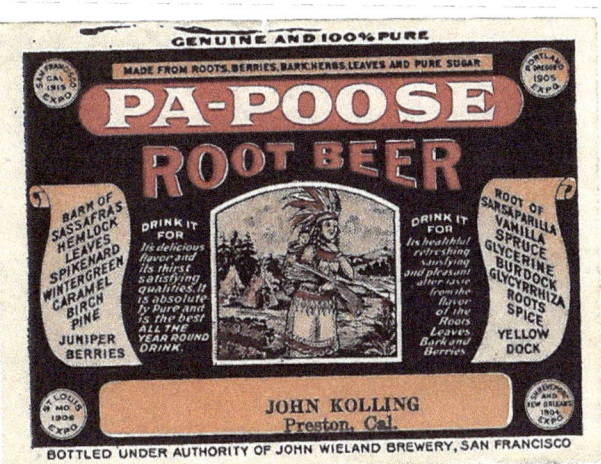

Prohibition

Prohibition

SAN FRANCISCO – JOHN WIELAND BREWERY
1856 – 1920
1932 – 1934 NP
Labels Prohibition

Prohibition   Prohibition

SAN JOSE – JOHN WIELAND BREWERY
PACIFIC BREWING & MALTING
1933-1951
Both Labels IRTP

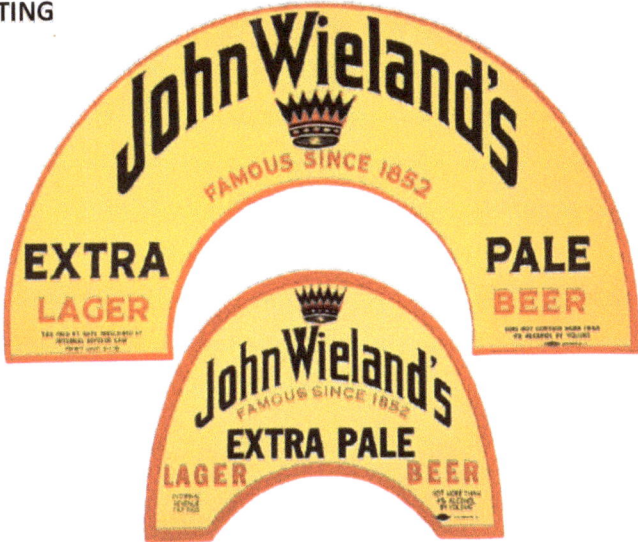

WIELAND KEG AND CASE LABELS

IRTP

IRTP

IRTP

IRTP

IRTP

SAN JOSE – JOHN WIELAND BREWERY
PACIFIC BREWING & MALTING CO.
1933-1951

IRTP

IRTP

IRTP

IRTP

IRTP

SAN FRANCISCO – JOHN WIELAND
1856 – 1920
Brewed and Bottled for Henry Weinhard Portland, Oregon
1932 – 1934 NP
Labels Pre-Prohibition

SAN FRANCISCO – JOHN WIELAND
1856 – 1920
1932 – 1934 NP
Top Label Jacob Adloff General Agent. Los Angeles Depot Pre-Prohibition
Red Wieland's Less Percent Label Prohibition
Blue Wieland Lager & Franciscaner Lager Labels Prohibition

SAN FRANCISCO – WASHINGTON BREWERY
1870 - 1916
Corrner Lombard & Taylor Streets
Labels Pre-Prohibition

Pre-Prohibition

SAN FRANCISCO – WUNDER BREWING CO.
1898 - 1909
PACIFIC CLUB
Label Pre-Prohibition

Pre-Prohibition

Pre-Prohibition

Pre-Prohibition

SAN FRANCISCO – WUNDER BREWING CO.
1898 - 1909
Top Label Brewed and Bottled for Wunder Bottling Co.
Bottom Label Brewed and Bottled for Wunder Bottling Co. Hanford Ice Co.
1932 – 1934 NP
Labels Pre-Prohibition

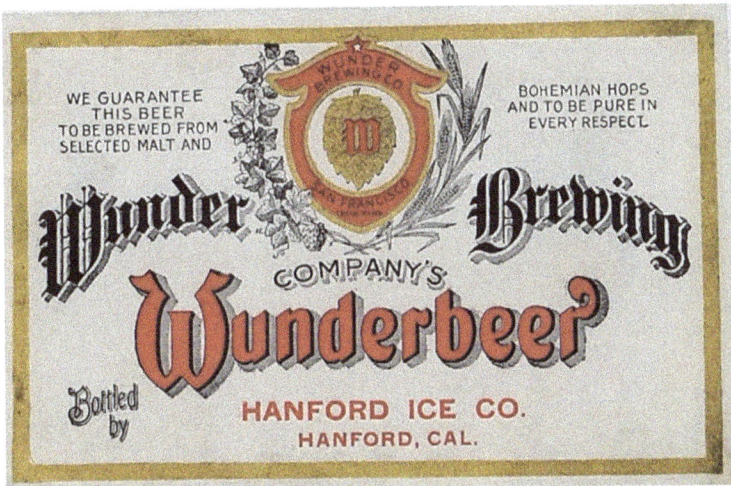

Pre-Prohibition   Pre-Prohibition

248

SAN JOSE - FREDERICKSBURG BREWING CO.
Cinnabar & Alameda Streets
1889 - 1920
L.) E. Scheuer & Co.
R.) Lang & Schmidt
Pre-Prohibition

Pre-Prohibition

Pre-Prohibition

Pre-Prohibition

Pre-Prohibition

Pre-Prohibition

SAN JOSE - FREDERICKSBURG BREWING CO.
Cinnabar & Alameda Streets
1889 - 1920
Pre-Prohibition

Pre-Prohibition

Pre-Prohibition

Pre-Prohibition

Pre-Prohibition

Pre-Prohibition

SAN JOSE - FREDERICKSBURG BREWING CO.
Cinnabar & Alameda Streets
1889 - 1920
Pre-Prohibition

Pre-Prohibition

Pre-Prohibition

Pre-Prohibition

IRTP

IRTP

SAN JOSE - FREDERICKSBURG BREWING CO.
Cinnabar & Alameda Streets
1889 - 1920
Label CA. U-Permit

IRTP

IRTP

IRTP

SAN JOSE - FREDERICKSBURG BREWING CO.
Cinnabar & Alameda Streets
1889 – 1920
Labels IRTP

IRTP

IRTP

IRTP

IRTP

SAN JOSE - FREDERICKSBURG BREWING CO.
Cinnabar & Alameda Streets
Top Left Label Bock
Top Right Label J. R. Luttrell & Son
Center Left Label C. Maurer & Sons
Center Right Label Maurer Bros.
1889 – 1920

SAN JOSE - FREDERICKSBURG BREWING CO.
Cinnabar & Alameda Streets
1889 - 1920
Top Label A. Mattei Fresno
Bottom labels Oakland Bottling Co.
Labels Pre-Prohibition

SAN JOSE – GARDEN CITY
Bassett & San Pedro Streets
1906 - 1920
Labels IRTP

IRTP

IRTP

IRTP

IRTP

SAN JOSE – GARDEN CITY
Bassett & San Pedro Streets
1906 - 1920
Labels IRTP

IRTP

IRTP

IRTP

IRTP

IRTP

SAN JOSE – PACIFIC BREWING AND MALTING CO.
1933 - 1951
Labels IRTP

SAN JOSE – PACIFIC BREWING AND MALTING CO.
1933 - 1951
Labels IRTP

SAN JOSE – PACIFIC BREWING AND MALTING CO.
1933 - 1951
Labels IRTP

IRTP

SAN JOSE – PACIFIC BREWING AND MALTING CO.
1933 - 1951
Labels IRTP

SAN JOSE – St. CLAIRE BREWING CO.
1090 West Salvador Street
1933 - 1940
Label Pre-Prohibition

IRTP

IRTP

Pre-Prohibition

IRTP

IRTP

SAN JOSE – ST. CLAIRE BREWERY CO.
1090 West Salvador
1933 – 1940
Labels IRTP

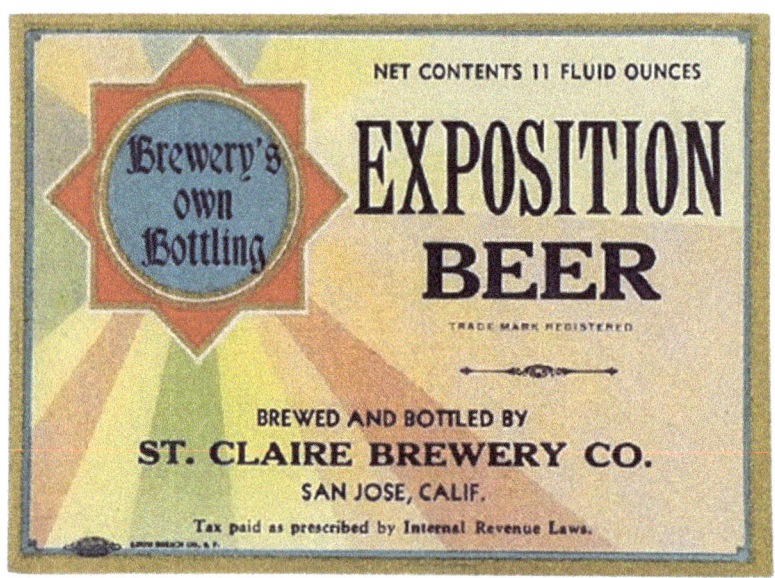

SAN JOSE – ST. CLAIRE BREWERY CO.
1090 West Salvador
1933 – 1940
Labels IRTP

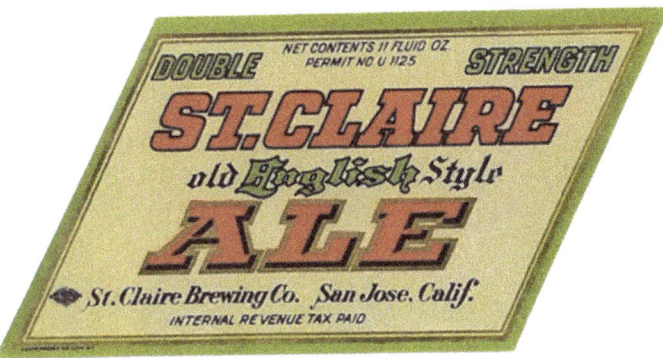

SAN JOSE – ST. CLAIRE BREWERY CO.
1090 West Salvador
1933 – 1940
Labels IRTP

SAN JOSE – ST. CLAIRE BREWERY CO.
1090 West Salvador
1933 – 1940
Labels IRTP

SAN JOSE – ST. CLAIRE BREWERY CO.
1090 West Salvador
1933 – 1940
Labels IRTP

SAN JOSE – ST. CLAIRE BREWERY CO.
1090 West Salvador
1933 – 1940
Labels IRTP

SANTA CRUZ – SANTA CRUZ BREWERY
Beck & Koehn Proprietors
Pre-Prohibition

BIG TREES BREWERY
MARKET STREET, SANTA CRUZ
Carl Beck sitting on wagon left side of buckboard with beard

SANTA CRUZ – SANTA CRUZ BREWERY
Label Pre-Prohibition
1906 - 1920

Pre-Prohibition **Pre-Prohibition**

SANTA CRUZ – SANTA CRUZ BREWERY
Labels Pre-Prohibition
1906 - 1920

SANTA CRUZ – SANTA CRUZ BREWERY
Labels Pre-Prohibition
1906 -1920

SANTA ROSA – GRACE BROS.
1897 – 1969
Labels Pre-Prohibition

Our Private Stock

SANTA ROSA – GRACE BROS.
1897 – 1969
Top Label CA. U-Permit
Bottom Label Pre-Prohibition

CA. U-Permit

Pre-Prohibition

SANTA ROSA – GRACE BROS.
1897 – 1969
Label CA. U-Permit

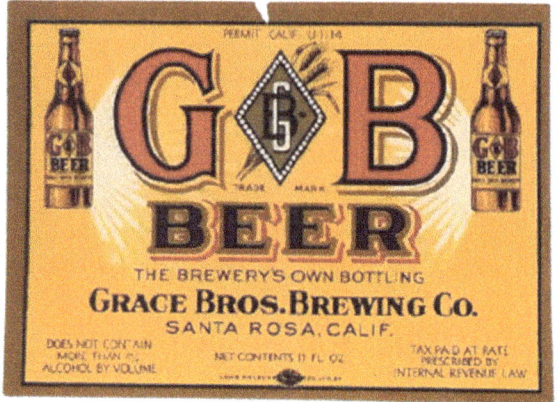

CA. U-Permit

CA. U-Permit

CA. U-Permit

IRTP

CA. U-Permit

SANTA ROSA – GRACE BROS.
1897 – 1969
Label IRTP

IRTP

IRTP

IRTP

IRTP

IRTP

SANTA ROSA – GRACE BROS.
1897 – 1969
Label IRTP

IRTP

IRTP

IRTP

IRTP

IRTP

SANTA ROSA – GRACE BROS.
1897 – 1969
Label IRTP

IRTP

IRTP

IRTP

IRTP

IRTP

SANTA ROSA – GRACE BROS.
1897 – 1969
Label IRTP

IRTP

IRTP   IRTP

IRTP
Guatemala Tax Stamp

SANTA ROSA – GRACE BROS.
1897 – 1969
Label IRTP

IRTP

IRTP

IRTP

IRTP

IRTP

SANTA ROSA – GRACE BROS.
1897 – 1969
Bottle Far Right
Cereal Beverage

Prohibition

Prohibition

1940's

1930's

Prohibition

SANTA ROSA – GRACE BROS.
1897 – 1969
Label Top Left CA. U-Permit
Other Labels IRTP

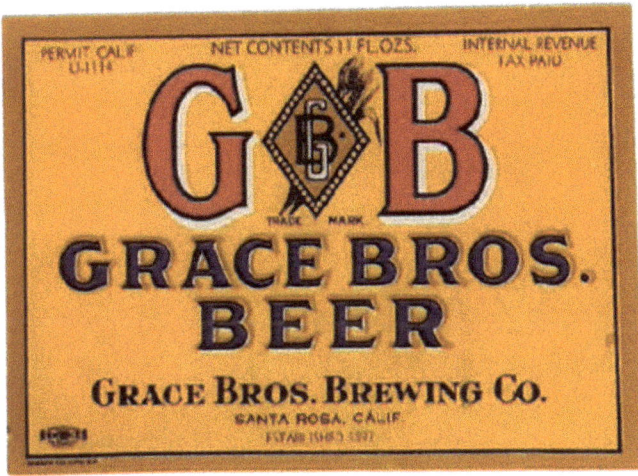

SANTA ROSA – GRACE BROS.
1897 – 1969
Labels IRTP

SANTA ROSA – GRACE BROS.
1897 – 1969
Labels IRTP

SANTA ROSA – GRACE BROS.
1897 – 1969
Labels IRTP

SANTA ROSA – NORTH BAY - GRACE BROS.
1942 – 1969
Label IRTP

IRTP

IRTP

IRTP

IRTP

IRTP

SANTA ROSA – SONOMA VALLEY BREWING CORPORATION
Dr. A. M. Buchner Vice-President & Brew Master
Former Brew Master at Albany Brewery in San Francisco
7 College Avenue
Label CA. U-Permit
1933 – 1935 NP

SONOMA - SONOMA BREWING CO.
Gottlier Kestler 1905 - 1908
Phillip Scheuer & John Steiner 1908
2nd Street East (North of Spain Street)
Agent for Buffalo Brewing Co.
Label Pre-Prohibition

Pre-Prohibition

STOCKTON – EL DORADO
1893 – 1920
1933 – 1955
Labels Pre-Prohibition

Pre-Prohibition

Pre-Prohibition

Pre-Prohibition

Prohibition

Pre-Prohibition

STOCKTON – EL DORADO BREWING CO.
1893 – 1920
1933 – 1955
Label Pre-Prohibition

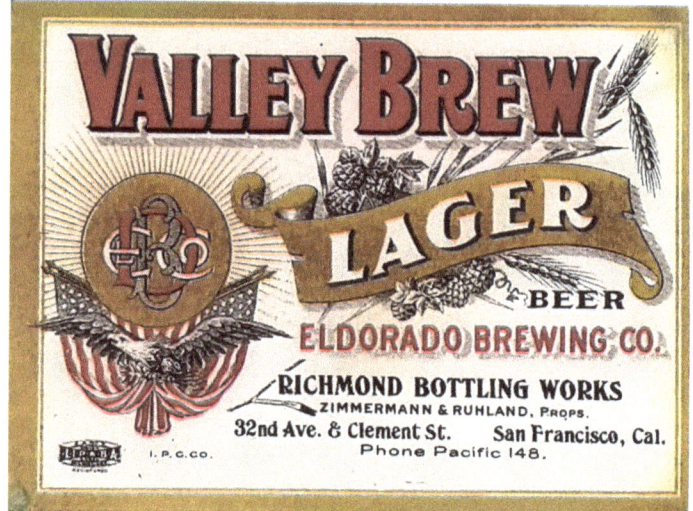

IRTP

IRTP

CA. U-Permit

Pre-Prohibition

CA. U-Permit

STOCKTON – EL DORADO BREWING CO.
1893 – 1920
1933 – 1955
Label Pre-Prohibition

CA. U-Permit

Pre-Prohibition

CA. U-Permit

CA. U-Permit

CA. U-Permit

STOCKTON – EL DORADO BREWING CO.
1893 – 1920
1933 – 1955
Labels IRTP

IRTP

Pre-Prohibition

STOCKTON – EL DORADO BREWING CO.
1893 – 1920
1933 – 1955
Label IRTP

IRTP

IRTP

Prohibition

Pre-Prohibition

IRTP

STOCKTON – EL DORADO BREWING CO.
1893 – 1920
1933 – 1955
Labels IRTP

IRTP   IRTP

IRTP

STOCKTON – EL DORADO BREWING CO.
1893 – 1920
1933 – 1955
Label Top Left IRTP
Label Top Right Prohibition
Center Label Pre-Prohibition
Bottom Labe CA. U-Permit

STOCKTON – EL DORADO BREWING CO.
1893 – 1920
1933 – 1955
Labels on Left Side Prohibition
Walderbush Beer Label Pre-Prohibition
Lisco Lager & London Tavern Stout Labels IRTP

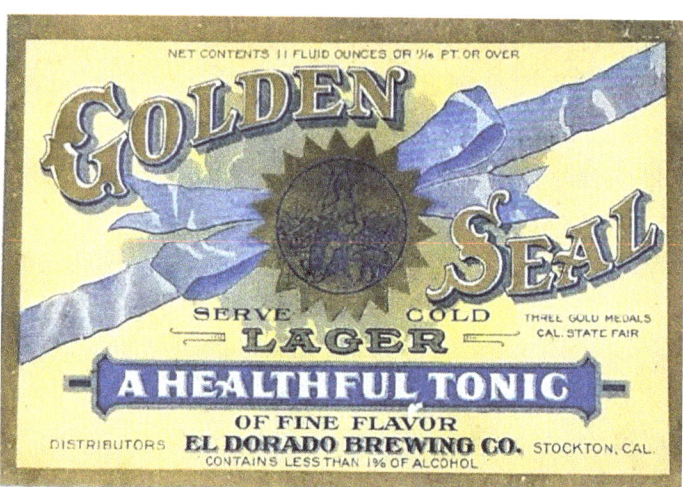
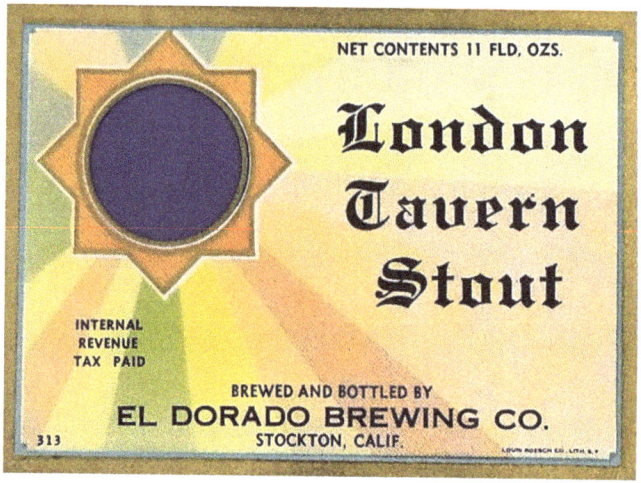

VALLEJO – SOLANO BREWING CO.
1904 - 1920
Label Pre-Prohibition

Pre-Prohibition

UKIAH – UKIAH BREWING & ICE Co.
1908 – 1920
Label Pre-Prohibition

Name	Pages
Acme Brewing Co. Los Angeles	19-20
Acme Brewing Co. San Francisco	111-124
Ahrens Bottling Co. Oakland	171
Albany Brewery – San Francisco	125
Albany Brewery – Hagemann	153
Albion Brewing San Francisco	126-130
Alpen Glow Beer San Francisco	165
Ambassador Brewing Co. Los Angeles	21-23
Anaheim Union Brewing Co.	1
Anchor Brewing Co. San Francisco	131
Annabelle Special Lager San Francisco	246
Appledorn's Bottling San Francisco	131
Argonaut Bottling San Francisco	163-164
Astor Wine Co. San Francisco	158
Asahi Wine Mfg. Co. San Francisco	154
August Lang Brewing San Francisco	155
Aztec Brewing Co. San Diego	99-109
Bakersfield Brewing Co.	2
Bakersfield - Kern Brewing Co.	3
Balboa Brewing Co. Los Angeles	24
Balboa Brewing Co. San Diego	110
Bavaria Brewery San Francisco	132
Beam & Randle-Wieland's San Francisco	245
Berkeley (West Berkeley) Raspiller	4
Blue and Gold Brewing Co. Oakland	61-62
Blue & Gold Brewing San Francisco	133
Boca Brewing Co.	232
Buffalo Brewing Co. Sacramento	81-89
Buffalo Brewing Co. Inc. Sacramento GB	90
Burgermeister Beer Milwaukee Brewery	165
Burgermeister Beer – San Francisco	212-213
California Brewing Assn. Napa	60
California Brewing Assn. San Francisco	113-122
California Brewing Co. Wieland's	233-244
Capital Brewing Co. Sacramento	91
Cascade Lager Beer San Francisco	175-176
Cascade Lager by Union San Francisco	229-230
Cervelli Bottling Co. San Francisco	119
Charles Wreden's Washington Brewery	246
City Brew & Bottling Co. San Francisco	156
Comet Distributing Co. Los Angeles	16
Consumers Brewing San Francisco	140-141
Consumers & North Star San Francisco	202-203
Cerveza Del Viejo Jose Garden City	167
Denver Bottling Co. San Francisco	158
Eagle Brewing Co. – San Francisco	134-135
Eastside Brewing Co. - Los Angeles	33-36
Eckert Brewing Co. – Los Angeles	25
E. H. Schade San Francisco	160-161
El Dorado Brewing Co. Stockton	288-295
El Rey Brewing Co. San Francisco	136-139
Enterprise Pioneer San Francisco	142
Enterprise Bottling Co. San Francisco	142-144
Etna Mills Brewery	5
Eureka - Humboldt Brewing Co.	6-7
Eureka - Humboldt Malt & Brewing Co.	8-10
Fauser & Co. San Francisco	155
Fauser & Co. Phoenix Beer San Francisco	172
Fauser & Co. St. Louis Beer San Francisco	172
Franciscaner by California Bottling Co.	245
Franco's Quality Beer San Jose	261
Fredericksburg Brewery San Jose	249-255
Fresno Brewing Co.	11
Fresno Brewing Co. Inc.	12-13
Fresno Brewing Co. Inc. (Grace)	14
Fresno Yosemite Brewing Co.	15
Garden City Brewing Co. San Francisco	163
Garden City Brewing Co. DBA San Jose	167
Garden City Cerveza Del Viejo Jose	167
Garden City Ritz Beer San Francisco	167
Garden City Ritz Steam Beer San Jose	256
Garden City Old Joe's Beer San Jose	257
General Brewing Corp. San Francisco	145-149
Globe Brewing Co. San Francisco	150-153
Golden State Brewery San Francisco	162-163
Golden West Brewing Co. Oakland	63-71
Grace Bros. Fresno Brewing Inc.	14
Grace Bros. Ltd. Los Ángeles	27-30
Grace Bros. Brewery Los Ángeles	30
Grace Bros. Inc. Sacramento	90
Grace Bros. Brewery Santa Rosa	273-285
Grace Bros. North Bay Santa Rosa	286
Gutsch Brewing Co. Inc Los Angeles	32
Hagemann Brewing Co. San Francisco	153
Henry Weinhard San Francisco	244
Hibernia Brewing Co. San Francisco	209
Hollywood Brewing Co.	16-17
Hollywood - Koch Brewing Co.	16
Home Brewing Co. Los Angeles	32
Hop Brew NA San Francisco	180
Hopsburger Beer San Francisco	175-176
Hopsburger by Union San Francisco	231-232
H. Rohrbacher Co. Stockton	181
Humboldt Brewing Co. Eureka	6-7
Humboldt Malt & Brewing Co. Eureka	8-10
Imperial Brewing Co. Los Ángeles	79
Jackson Brewing Co. San Francisco	154
Jackson - John Strohm Brewery	18
Japan Brewing Co. San Francisco	155
John Fauser & Co. San Francisco	159
John Fauser & Co. San Francisco	177
John Wieland Brewery San Francisco	233-241
John Weiland's Brewery San Jose	242-243
John Weiland's Brewery San Francisco	244-245
Joseph Schwartz Brewing San Francisco	179
Kern Brewing Co. Bakersfield	3

Name	Page
Koch Brewing Co. Hollywood	16
Leidig's Pilsner Style Beer Salinas	205
Liberty Bottling Co. San Francisco	159
Los Angeles - Los Angeles Brewing Co.	33-36
Lynwood Brewing Co. Lynwood	57
Maier Brewing Co. Los Angeles	38-43
Mathie Brewing Co. Los Angeles	44
Milwaukee Brewing Co. San Francisco	157-167
Milwaukee Beer San Francisco	164
Milwaukee Brewery San Jose	167
Mission Brewing Co. Los Angeles	37
Mission Brewing Co. San Diego	110
Modesto Brewery Inc. Modesto	58-59
Molakadis Bros. Bottlers San Francisco	156
Monarch Brewing Co. Los Angeles	45-47
Monterey Brewing Co. Los Angeles	48
Monterey Brewing Co. Salinas	96-97
Mt. Baldy Brewing Co. Los Angeles	31
Mt. Wilson Brewing Co. Los Angeles	31
Napa Valley Brewing Co. Napa	60
National Bottling Works San Francisco	169-172
National Brewing Co. San Francisco	168-169
North Bay Brewery Santa Rosa GB	286
North Star Brewery San Francisco	173-174
O-MY-Brewing Co. Los Angeles	43
Oakland Brewing & Malting Co.	61-62
Old Dutch Brew Co. San Francisco	174
Old German Lager San Francisco	170
Old Heidelbrau San Francisco	171
Old Lager Brewing Co. San Francisco	175
Old Saxon Products San Francisco	156
Old Time Brewing Corporation Rosemead	80
Olympia Brewing Co. San Francisco	176
Olympus Lager Beer San Francisco	156
Oxnard – Charles Peverley	74
Pacific Brewing Co. San Francisco	95
Pacific Brewing Co. San Francisco	199
Pacific Brewing & Malting San Francisco	176
Pacific Brewing & Malting San Jose	242-243
Pacific Brewing & Malting Co. San Jose	258-261
Perfection Beer San Francisco	157-158
Pioneer - Enterprise San Francisco	142
Phoenix Beer San Francisco	177
Rainier Brewing Co. Los Angeles	49
Raspiller Brewing Co. West Berkeley	4
Red Bluff Brewing Co. Red Bluff	75
Red Bluff United States Brewing Co.	76-78
Rainier Brewing Co. San Francisco	182-198
Rainier Sales Co. Paso Robles	23
Regal Amber Brewing Co. San Francisco	205-210
Regal Products San Francisco	204
Rio Brewing Co. Los Angeles	49
Rishwain Bros. Stockton	210
Rollinson Brewery Los Angeles	50
Rosemead Imperial Brewing Co.	79
Rosemead Olde Tyme Brewing Corp.	80
Ruthstaller City Brewery Sacramento	82
Saint Claire Brewing Co. San Jose	262-268
Salinas Brewing Co.	92
Salinas Brewing & Ice Co.	93-95
Salinas Monterey Brewing Co.	96-98
San Diego Brewing Co.	109
San Francisco Brewing Corp.	178
San Francisco Brewing Corporation	211-227
Santa Anita Beer Co. Los Angeles	31
Santa Clara Brewery (St. Claire)	125
Santa Cruz Brewery Image	269
Santa Cruz Brewing Co.	270-272
Santa Rosa Grace Bros.	273-285
Santa Rosa North Bay Grace Bros.	286
Santa Rosa Sonoma Valley Brewing Co.	287
Shasta Brand Beer Oakland	74
Solano Brewing Co. Vallejo	296
Sonoma Brewing Co. Sonoma	287
Sonoma Valley Brewing Santa Rosa	287
Southern Brewing Co. Los Angeles	51
Standard Brewing Corp. Sacramento	91
Stewart McKee & Co. Los Angeles	26
Stockton El Dorado Brewing Co.	288-295
Supreme Home Brew San Francisco	180
Tacoma Brewery San Francisco	200-201
Tivoli Beer Los Angeles	26
Tornberg's Consumer San Francisco	131-132
Tru-Blu Beer San Francisco Brewing Co	178
Ukiah Brewing & Ice Co.	297
United States Brewing Co. Red Bluff	76-78
U. S. Brewery & Malt San Francisco	181
Union Brewing Co. Anaheim	1
Union Brewing & Malt San Francisco	228-230
Union Brewing Co. San Francisco	231-232
Vallejo Solano Brewing Co.	296
Valley Brew Stockton	288-295
Vernon Brewing Co. Los Angeles	52-54
Viking Brewery San Francisco	181
Washington Brewery San Francisco	246
Weiland's Brewery San Francisco	233-241
Weiland's Brewery San Jose	242-243
Weiland's Brewery San Francisco	244-245
West Berkeley Brewery (Raspiller)	4
West Coast Breweries Los Angeles	55-56
W. R. Grace Label San Francisco	156
Wunder Brewing Co. Oakland	72-73
Wunder Brewing Co. San Francisco	247-248
X.L. Brewing Co. Inc. Los Angeles	31
Yosemite Brewing Co. Fresno	15
Zobelein & Maier Los Angeles	33-36

OTHER TITLES BY JOHN C. BURTON

GRACE BROS. BREWERIES, HISTORY & MEMORABILIA
SANTA ROSA - LOS ANGELES – SACRAMENTO - FRESNO

By John C. Burton

With Major Contributions by
Rawley Douglas - John Cartwright
James Arietta Bob Welch
Cathy Grace-Hayes

GRACE BROS. BREWERIES & HISTORY
SANTA ROSA - LOS ANGELES – SACRAMENTO - FRESNO

A guide and reference not just of their empire in the beer business but also includes their numerous ventures including an ice house, cold storage business, the DeTurk Winery, the dairy business, their land and ranches throughout California and being a major retailer of refrigerators during and after Prohibition.

LAKE, NAPA, SONOMA, MENDOCINO, SOLANO,
And HUMBOLDT MINERAL & HOT SPRINGS

By John C. Burton & John Louder
Cover compliments of Witherell Auctions, Sacramento Ca.

LAKE, NAPA, SONOMA, MENDOCINO, SOLANO,
And HUMBOLDT MINERAL & HOT SPRINGS

Pine Mountain Mineral Water label
John Burton collection

Bartlett reverse-on-glass compliments
Richard Siri collection

OTHER TITLES BY JOHN C. BURTON

SONOMA COUNTY DRUGGISTS

Featuring Advertising, Bottles, Medicine Glasses, Photographs and Local History

Maynard's Drug Store, Petaluma, circa 1900

Frank A. Sternad and John C. Burton

SONOMA COUNTY DRUGGISTS
PHARMACY, PROPRIETARY & DRUG STORE BOTTLES
Featuring Bottles, Advertising & Dose Glasses

 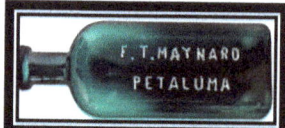

  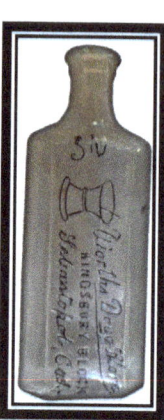

SAN RAFAEL - SAUSALITO – SAN ANSELMO
SODA, SELTZER, BEER, AND SPIRITS BOTTLES

A GUIDE AND REFERENCE TO BOTTLERS OF BEER, SODA, SELTZER, AND SPIRITS OF MARIN COUNTY INCLUDING A LISTING OF ANTIQUE BOTTLES

By John C. Burton & John Louder

SAN RAFAEL - SAUSALITO – SAN ANSELMO
SODA, SELTZER, BEER, AND SPIRITS BOTTLES

A GUIDE AND REFERENCE TO BOTTLERS OF BEER, SODA, SELTZER, AND SPIRITS OF MARIN COUNTY INCLUDING A LISTING OF ANTIQUE BOTTLES

SAN RAFAEL SODA WORKS P & B PROP'S
courtesy of American Bottle Auctions
Ell-Ell WHISKEY MARIN COUNTY courtesy
of American Bottle Auctions
EDDIE GOLDEN paper-mâché pint flask
John Louder collection

www.ingramcontent.com/pod-product-compliance
Lightning Source LLC
Chambersburg PA
CBHW061118070526
44583CB00028B/3329